FREE INDEED

Published by Legacy Press
www.legacypress.org
Your life tells a story; we can help you write it.

info@JTerryMoore.org
c/o International Apostolic Network
4041 Marsh Lane
Carrollton, TX 75007

Cover and interior design and layout by Nelly Murariu @PixBeeDesign.com

Cover and interior images are the property of Shutterstock and their respective copyright owners.

Free Indeed

Discovering Wholeness & Victory in Christ

TERRY MOORE

CONTENTS

Acknowledgments   vii
Introduction   ix

1: Love, Identity, and Purpose   1

2: Receiving and Embracing the Holy Spirit   19

3: The Battleground   33

4: Unlocking Important Truths   45

5: Generational Patterns   59

6: Ungodly Beliefs and Strongholds   77

7: Setting Our Minds on the Right Things   87

8: Trauma and Inner Healing   97

9: Realm of Darkness   107

10: Daily Walking it Out   121

Appendices
APPENDIX A: Your True Identity as a Believer   129
APPENDIX B: Freedom from the Flesh   135
APPENDIX C: Declaration of Faith   139
APPENDIX D: Healing the Brokenhearted   141

Resource List   143
About the Author   145
More Titles Available in the Advanced Foundations Series   147

ACKNOWLEDGMENTS

It was after a life-changing encounter with the Holy Spirit at a James Robison meeting in 1982 that I, my wife Susan, and some friends, began a journey of discovering freedom that can only be received through a relationship with Jesus Christ. I learned about the power of the Holy Spirit that is available to all believers to empower us to live an abundant life.

Though I had spent most of my life attending church, it was in that meeting that my eyes were opened, and I realized there was an enemy of my soul, and he was taking me captive. I believe God wants everyone to experience this revelation so they can understand how to walk in Freedom.

It is my prayer that this book will help you to know how the enemy is working in your life, and what you can do to be free in Christ.

I want to thank James and Betty Robison for their friendship and allowing God to use them to speak the truth so that Susan and I could experience this freedom. I also want to recognize Brad and Betsy Burns, who have been friends since our college days. They were part of the original church, and I am thankful for their support as we have led Sojourn Church together.

I remain thankful to my beautiful wife, Susan, of 48 years and our children, David and Meredith. They have seen the changes in my life because of these truths. It is our prayer that you encounter the love of God and His freedom as you read these pages.

INTRODUCTION

When Jesus began His earthly ministry, He preached the Kingdom of God, and He demonstrated the Kingdom of God by casting out demons and healing the sick (Matthew 4:17, 23, 24). He demonstrated the Kingdom by literally "setting the captives free" in every way—spiritually, mentally, emotionally, and physically. He taught His disciples about the power of the Kingdom while demonstrating that the same power and authority was theirs. His instructed them to follow His example and train up more disciples to do the same (Matthew 9:1-8); to go into all the world and make disciples (Matthew 28:18-20). Not only did Jesus set the captives free, but He went to the Cross and paid with His life in order to secure His victory for us, for all eternity.

Luke 4:18-19 describes Jesus's earthly ministry: "'The Spirit of the Lord is upon Me, because He has anointed Me to preach the gospel to the poor; he has sent Me to heal the brokenhearted, to proclaim liberty to the captives and recovery of sight to the blind, to set at liberty those who are oppressed; to proclaim the acceptable year of the Lord.'"

He then announced in Luke 4:21, "Today this Scripture is fulfilled in your hearing."

Because "Jesus Christ is the same yesterday, today, and forever" (Hebrews 13:8), He is still ministering today by the power of the Holy Spirit (Luke 4:18-19). We can experience His freedom, wholeness; and, as His disciples, participate with the Holy Spirit in ministering Luke 4:18-19 to others.

Even though Jesus has paid *in full* for our freedom, there are still many who are not living victoriously in His freedom. Jesus promised us freedom in John 8:31-32: "Then Jesus said to those Jews who believed Him, 'If you abide in My word, you are My disciples indeed. And you shall know the truth, and the truth shall make you free.'"

Why does the truth make us free? Because the truth is not a set of rules or principles. Truth is a person. It is Jesus, the living Word. As we come to know Him, to know His Word, and choose to put our faith in Him and fully embrace the Holy Spirit, who leads us into truth, we will be set free. If the truth makes us free, then believing and acting upon a lie will keep us in bondage. Many people are still in bondage. Why? Because either they do not know the truth, or they do not believe the truth.

God paid a very costly price for our freedom, but that was not His only purpose for Jesus's death on the cross. He wants us to be conformed to His image and become His sons and daughters (Romans 8:29). It's a process that often must be worked into our lives over time. It's not a "quick fix." But in the waiting, in the pressing, the growing, and the healing, we can take delight and be encouraged as we stand strong and run the race with endurance. Surely, the ultimate gift of freedom is so worth it! I trust that the principles outlined within these pages will lead you to new levels of understanding and freedom!

Below are just some of the topics we will be discussing in depth in order to prepare your heart and give you a sense of the journey that awaits:

- † Foundation of Freedom – accepting the love of the Father and your identity as His child

- † Power of Freedom – receiving and embracing the Holy Spirit and His purpose

- † Standing for Freedom – waging war against the forces of darkness

- † Keys to Freedom – giving your whole heart to God and taking personal responsibility

† Doors to Freedom – dealing with strongholds and recurring issues

† Purpose of Freedom – helping others to become free

† Securing Freedom – laying aside the "old man" and holding fast to new life

Freedom Begins with Receiving Jesus

True *Freedom* begins at the Cross with receiving Jesus Christ as your Lord and Savior. John 3:16 says, "For God so loved the world, that He gave His only begotten Son that whoever believes in Him should not perish but have everlasting life." 1 John 1:9 says, "If we confess our sins, He is faithful and just to forgive us our sins and to cleanse us from all unrighteousness." If you have not believed in Jesus and accepted Him as your Savior and Lord, take a moment right now to give your life to Him by praying this prayer:

> *"Heavenly Father, I bow before all of Heaven and earth and confess my sin and my need for a Savior. Jesus, I believe You are the Son of God and that You took my sin upon You, so that I can become your righteousness and have a life in eternity with You and all the saints. I ask You to cleanse me from sin and I give my life to You. Thank You for saving me and leading me. In Jesus name, Amen."*

If you have prayed this prayer for the very first time, welcome to the Kingdom of God! It's the most important decision of your life. You will want to become involved in a Bible-believing church where you can grow, be encouraged, be baptized, make new friends, and walk out your new life in Christ with other believers.

I pray that as you read through this book, you will find true freedom and come to know in great measure the "grace of the Lord Jesus Christ, and the love of God, and the communion of the Holy Spirit" (2 Corinthians 13:14).

And... "that the God of our Lord Jesus Christ, the Father of glory, may give to you the spirit of wisdom and revelation in the knowledge of Him, the eyes of your understanding being enlightened; that you may know what is the hope of His calling, what are the riches of the glory of His inheritance in the saints, and what is the exceeding greatness of His power toward us who believe, according to the working of His mighty power" (Ephesians 1:17-19).

Terry Moore

Founding Pastor and Elder, Sojourn Church, Carrollton, TX
Founder and President, International Apostolic Network,
JTerryMoore.org

Love, Identity, and Purpose

FOUNDATION OF FREEDOM

Experts in the field of counseling and ministry tell us that everyone struggles with issues of *love, identity,* and *purpose.* We seem to be born with an inherent need to know and feel that we are loved, a need to know who we really are, and a need to understand why we were born and what we are supposed to do with our lives.

Let's look at a Scripture in the Bible from Genesis 1:26-28: "Then God said, 'Let Us make man in Our image, according to Our likeness; let them have dominion over the fish of the sea, over the birds of the air, and over the cattle, over all the earth and over every creeping thing that creeps on the earth.' So, God created man in His own image; in the image of God He created him; male and female He created them. Then God blessed them, and God said to them, 'Be fruitful and multiply; fill the earth and subdue it; have dominion over the fish of the sea, over the birds of the air, and over every living thing that moves on the earth.'"

This passage speaks to these three, very real concerns that are so important to us and to God. Genesis 1:26 clearly shows that we were created in God's image; and, since God is love, this speaks of His love for us. It also reveals that God created us in His likeness, His image, which gives us our identity. Then in Genesis 1:28, our purpose is clearly defined, which is to "be fruitful and multiply; fill the earth and subdue it; have dominion." In the New Testament, this means to advance the Kingdom of God.

But in a life—altering moment in time, things changed. The man that God had created and had given love, identity, and purpose to ... *sinned*. Adam and Eve willfully chose to disobey God and ate from the "tree of the knowledge of good and evil." The result was that they immediately became aware of their brokenness, their shame, their nakedness and their eyes were opened to the full weight of sin.

"Then the eyes of both of them were opened, and they knew that they were naked; and they sewed fig leaves together and made themselves coverings. And they heard the sound of the Lord God walking in the garden in the cool of the day, and Adam and his wife hid themselves from the presence of the Lord God among the trees of the garden. Then the Lord God called to Adam and said to him, 'Where are you?' So, he said, 'I heard Your voice in the garden, and I was afraid because I was naked; and I hid myself.'" And He said, "Who told you that you were naked? Have you eaten from the tree of which I commanded you that you should not eat?" Then the man said, 'The woman whom You gave to be with me, she gave me of the tree, and I ate'" (Genesis 3:7-12).

They became self-focused and uncomfortable in who they were; they became aware of their shame. They lost their identity; and, when they heard the Lord calling to them, they were afraid and hid themselves from the presence of God. Fear came into their hearts—a clear indication that they believed they had lost the love of the Father. When confronted with their actions, they blamed each other and would not take personal responsibility for their sin. As a result of their sin, their relationship with God was broken, and we know they were cast out of the garden, and experienced separation from their loving Father. It continues today in every man, woman, and child. The result is that we are spiritual orphans. But there is HOPE!

Restored Love, Identity, and Purpose

The wonderful truth is that God never changed His mind about who we are and who He wants us to be. From the beginning of time, He has remained faithful to His original design for us. Though we lost our favored position through the fall in the garden (Genesis 3), the good news is that Jesus took our place and became as an orphan, in order that we could return to full sonship as a child of God. He made a way for us to be restored and know His love through the Cross. Now we can discover our identity as sons and daughters of God and fulfil our purpose of advancing His Kingdom. It's completely ours, if we will only receive it.

Spiritual sons and daughters are celebrated, welcomed home to the Father's house, and spend their lives working together with Him. Sons don't work toward achieving success because everything in the Father's Kingdom is theirs. Sons cooperate with the Father in what He is doing. Remember, as a Son, Jesus announced that, He could do only what He sees His father doing, because whatever the Father does the Son also does." (John 5:19 NIV) "I only do what I see My Father doing, and I only say what I hear My Father say."

The Love of the Father

Receiving the love of the Father is one of the most important, life-changing experiences that can happen to anyone, and it is a crucial step on the way to freedom and wholeness. Living in a deep revelation of God's love establishes a foundation in our lives that neither the enemy nor man can shake. Knowing His love is not just gaining information, which is important, but it's the revelation and daily involvement of the Holy Spirit, who makes the love of the Father real in our lives in a personal and intimate way. If we ask, He will reveal His love to us (Romans 8:15-16).

Receiving and living in the love of the Father is one of the primary areas in our lives where the devil attacks with lies and deception. The devil wants us to believe that God is angry with us when, in fact, God loves us so much that He gave His only Son to die for us (John 3:16). The love of the Father brings us into complete acceptance and forgiveness of sin. It causes us to enter into His presence and experience an intimacy with Him that is beyond anything we have ever encountered.

"Living in a deep revelation of God's love establishes a foundation in our lives that neither the enemy nor man can shake."

He wants you to experience the fullness of His love for you. He is on your side no matter what you are up against and He is there to answer when you ask Him to show you His heart for you. The following verses speak of the truth of God's love. I encourage you to spend some time with these verses, meditate on them, and even memorize them. Speak out these words and do the same with other Scriptures about God's love. As you meditate on the Word, the Holy Spirit will speak to your heart and give you a life-changing revelation of the Father's love.

> "For God so loved the world that He gave His only begotten Son, that whoever believes in Him should not perish but have everlasting life." John 3:16

> "But God, who is rich in mercy, because of His great love with which He loved us, even when we were dead in trespasses, made us alive together with Christ (by grace you have been saved)..." Ephesians 2:4-5

> "But God demonstrates His own love toward us, in that while we were still sinners, Christ died for us." Romans 5:8

> "In this the love of God was manifested toward us, that God has sent His only begotten Son into the world, that we might

live through Him. In this is love, not that we loved God, but that He loved us and sent His Son to be the propitiation for our sins." 1 John 4:9, 10

"He who did not spare His own Son, but delivered Him up for us all, how shall He not with Him also freely give us all things?" Romans 8:32

How We See God

One key to receiving the love of the Father is to make sure that we have an accurate perception of the Father. If we have a distorted image of God, we will struggle to truly receive His love. Jimmy Evans writes, "There is a direct parallel between how we viewed our parents, especially our earthly father, and how we view God." The following is adapted from his book, *Freedom From Your Past* (p.131). Use it as a tool to help you determine where your perception of God may be distorted and whether you have projected some of these characteristics on to Him.

BEHAVIOR OF PARENT	MISCONCEPTION ABOUT GOD
Legalistic; harsh disciplinarian	God is mad; demanding; impersonal
Perfectionist; high standards; little praise	God is never satisfied; disappointed in me
Little or no affection	God is impersonal; distant
Critical; verbally abusive	God is angry; doesn't really love people
Workaholic; focused outside the family	God is detached; I'm not important to Him
Abusive; dominating	God rules by fear; cannot really be trusted
Moody; temperamental	God is unpredictable; doesn't always love
Sinful; poor discipline; bad behavior	God is a pushover; too nice
Doting; spoiling; smothering	God exists for me and my desires
Compared you to siblings and other children; showed favoritism	God has favorites; loves some people more than others; loves based on performance
Made promises and broke them; didn't follow through on warnings; inconsistent	God is unreliable; His Word cannot be trusted
Hypocritical	God isn't relevant or powerful

Getting the Correct View of God

For us to get the correct view of God, we must look at Jesus. In John 14:9, Jesus tells us that in seeing Him, we have seen the Father. Therefore, we must spend time reading the gospel accounts of Jesus in Matthew, Mark, Luke, and John. Let's look at some examples from Scripture of Jesus showing us the Father.

> "Jesus said to him, 'Have I been with you so long, and yet you have not known Me, Philip? He who has seen Me has seen the Father; so how can you say, 'Show us the Father'?'" John 14:9

> "He is the image of the invisible God, the firstborn over all creation. For by Him all things were created that are in Heaven and that are on earth, visible and invisible, whether thrones or dominions or principalities or powers. All things were created through Him and for Him. And He is before all things, and in Him all things consist. And He is the head of the body, the church, who is the beginning, the firstborn from the dead, that in all things He may have the preeminence." Colossians 1:15-18

The following is the story of the woman caught in adultery and brought before Jesus. Note that in this Father/daughter moment, Jesus demonstrates the unconditional love of the Father by not judging her. Instead, he offers love, healing, and restoration:

> "But Jesus went to the Mount of Olives. Now early in the morning He came again into the temple, and all the people came to Him; and He sat down and taught them. Then the scribes and Pharisees brought to Him a woman caught in adultery. And when they had set her in the midst, they said to Him, 'Teacher, this woman was caught in adultery, in the very act. Now Moses, in the law, commanded us that such should be stoned. But what do You say?' This they said, testing Him,

that they might have something of which to accuse Him. But Jesus stooped down and wrote on the ground with His finger, as though He did not hear.

So, when they continued asking Him, He raised Himself up and said to them, 'He who is without sin among you, let him throw a stone at her first.' And again He stooped down and wrote on the ground. Then those who heard it, being convicted by their conscience, went out one by one, beginning with the oldest even to the last. And Jesus was left alone, and the woman standing in the midst. When Jesus had raised Himself up and saw no one but the woman, He said to her, 'Woman, where are those accusers of yours? Has no one condemned you?'

She said, 'No one, Lord.'

And Jesus said to her, 'Neither do I condemn you; go and sin no more.'

Then Jesus spoke to them again, saying, 'I am the light of the world. He who follows Me shall not walk in darkness but have the light of life.'" John 8:1-12

Another powerful example of the Father's love is found in Luke 15:11-32, *The Parable of the Lost Son*. The lost son returns to the father feeling totally unworthy and ashamed, unable to embrace the truth of his full inheritance. The older son was self-focused, felt entitled, and totally rejected. But this earthly father demonstrates his absolute love for both of his sons.

Please take time to read this wonderful account and reflect upon the true heart that God the Father has for us—His beloved sons and daughters.

As you pray, focus on the following steps:

Steps to Receiving God's Love

- † Know the truth that God loves you by studying the Word.

- † Get the correct image of God through reading and studying Jesus.

- † Receive the Spirit of Adoption which makes the Love of the Father real.

- † Forgive your earthly father for what he did or didn't do.

- † Forgive yourself for all of your failures.

- † Receive God's perfect love that casts out fear.

- † Release control.

"For this reason I bow my knees to the Father of our Lord Jesus Christ, from whom the whole family in heaven and earth is named, that He would grant you, according to the riches of His glory, to be strengthened with might through His Spirit in the inner man, that Christ may dwell in your hearts through faith; that you, being rooted and grounded in love, may be able to comprehend with all the saints what is the width and length and depth and height—to know the love of Christ which passes knowledge; that you may be filled with all the fullness of God. Now to Him who is able to do exceedingly abundantly above all that we ask or think, according to the power that works in us, to Him be glory in the church by Christ Jesus to all generations, forever and ever. Amen." Ephesians 3:14-20

Identity

Once we have discovered God's awesome love for us, it's central to our being to realize that we are not simply loved and forgiven, but also "accepted in the Beloved" as sons and daughters of God (Ephesians 1:6).

Is your identity framed by your past failures or your past experiences? We often get our identity from the way we see ourselves. Many times, the way in which we see ourselves is the way the devil wants us to see ourselves. Our enemy is always attacking who we are—telling us that we are unloved, unwanted, a mistake, or some other lie. The devil challenged God's Word to Jesus in Luke 4, and he will challenge you.

How we see ourselves dramatically affects how we relate to God and others.

How we see ourselves dramatically affects how we relate to God and others. Are you a sinner saved by grace, or a saint, a son of God? If you see yourself as a saint, your behavior will reflect that. Likewise, if you see yourself as a sinner, you will reflect that behavior as well.

So how do you see yourself?

We must believe the Truth—I am who God says that I am; I am worth what God paid for me. I am His beloved son/daughter. It is time that we see ourselves from His perspective. We are truly in a place of *favor* with God. We are literally "friends" of God (John 15:12-15). We discover who we really are as we find out who we are *in Christ* and who He is in us. His Word is absolutely clear: we are a new creation in Christ, and this is our true identity. He really does make us new! The following verses are taken from the Word of God which speak about our identity and position in the Lord.

(Listed in *Appendix A*, you will find additional Scriptures for further study and reflection, that will reveal who we truly are in Christ. Take some time to read over them, as well.)

> "I do not pray for these alone, but also for those who will believe in Me through their word; that they all may be one, as You, Father, are in Me, and I in You; that they also may be one in Us, that the world may believe that You sent Me. And the glory which You gave Me I have given them, that they may be one just as We are one: I in them, and You in Me; that they may be made perfect in one, and that the world may know that You have sent Me, and have loved them as You have loved Me." John 17:20-23

> "Behold what manner of love the Father has bestowed on us, that we should be called children of God! Therefore the world does not know us, because it did not know Him." I John 3:1

> "Therefore if anyone is in Christ, he is a new creation; old things have passed away; behold, all things have become new." 2 Corinthians 5:17

> "And because you are sons, God has sent forth the Spirit of His Son into your hearts, crying out, 'Abba, Father!' Therefore you are no longer a slave but a son, and if a son, then an heir of God through Christ." Galatians 4:6, 7

> "To the praise of the glory of His grace, by which He made us accepted in the Beloved. In Him we have redemption through His blood, the forgiveness of sins, according to the riches of His grace." Ephesians 1:6, 7

Steps to Receiving Identity

† Know and believe the truth of who Jesus says you are.

† Study Scripture and identify passages that speak to who the Bible says you are.

† Write down these Scriptures and refer to them often or when you are in doubt.

† Reject all negative perceptions about yourself—the past, your actions, or failures.

† Receive fully and embrace the Holy Spirit, who brings truth about your identity.

† Talk with God and ask Him to share with you how He sees you, His beloved.

Purpose

In addition to receiving a revelation of the Father's awesome love and an understanding of our identity in Him, we must find God's purpose for our lives. God has a specific and perfect plan for your life, which you will discover as you continue to walk close to Him. All of us, however, have a corporate purpose as children of God—to advance His Kingdom. Genesis 1:28 describes the ministry of advancing God's Kingdom: "Be fruitful and multiply; fill the earth and subdue it; and have dominion over the fish of the sea, over the birds of the air, and over every living thing that moves on the earth."

The New Testament encourages us in this same ministry in Romans 8:17, which tells us that our purpose is to be "heirs of God and joint heirs with Christ." We advance His Kingdom by joining Him in His ministry of setting the captives free (Luke 4:18,19), representing Him on Earth.

The Great Commission is one of the most significant passages in the Holy Bible. First, it's the last recorded personal instruction given by Jesus to His disciples. Second, it's a special calling from Jesus Christ to all His followers to take specific action while on this earth. The Great Commission is found in the Gospel of Matthew 28:18-20: "Jesus came and spoke to them saying, 'All authority has been given to Me in heaven and on earth. Go therefore and make disciples of all the nations, baptizing them in the name of the Father and of the Son and of the Holy Spirit, teaching them to observe all things that I have commanded you and lo, I am with you always, even to the end of the age.'"

> *"Then He called His twelve disciples together and gave them power and authority over all demons, and to cure diseases. He sent them to preach the Kingdom of God and to heal the sick."*

Also, in Luke 9:1-2, we read, "Then He called His twelve disciples together and gave them power and authority over all demons, and to cure diseases. He sent them to preach the Kingdom of God and to heal the sick."

Jesus calls every Christian to step out in faith and spread the Good News. This is faith in action! People who obey this command change their spiritual lives forever. As you walk in the power and authority given to you by Christ, you will see amazing things happen and you will be a part of advancing His Kingdom *on earth as it is in Heaven*!

Jesus's Crises in Love, Identity, and Purpose

It's interesting to see and take note of the fact that Jesus had to face His own crises and attacks in the areas of love, identity, and purpose. We read in the following passage that Jesus was baptized with water because it was important for Him to do this. As He prayed, the Holy Spirit came upon Him. Luke 3:21-22 says, "When all the people were baptized, it came to pass that Jesus also was baptized; and while He prayed, the Heaven was opened. And the Holy Spirit descended in bodily form like a dove upon Him, and a voice came from Heaven which said, 'You are My beloved Son; in You I am well pleased.'" He was literally birthed by the power of the Holy Spirit.

There is importance in reviewing what happened with Christ at this point. The Holy Spirit came upon Him to endue Him with power to do the ministry He was sent to do (Luke 4:18-19). The Father spoke from Heaven and said, "You are My beloved Son; in You I am well pleased." Did Jesus need the Father's affirmation? No. As God, He doesn't need anything, but as man and as an example for us, He needed to receive the Father's affirmation. If Jesus needed this, how much more do we need this?

Immediately following in Luke 4:1-3, we read that Jesus was led by the Holy Spirit into the wilderness: "Then Jesus, being filled with the Holy Spirit, returned from the Jordan and was led by the Spirit into the wilderness, being tempted for forty days by the devil. And in those days He ate nothing, and afterward, when they had ended, He was hungry. And the devil said to Him, 'If You are the Son of God, command this stone to become bread.'"

The series of temptations that Jesus underwent at the hand of the enemy, the devil, was meant to challenge the words the Father had spoken to the Son just forty days before: "If you are the Son of God..."—the devil continued to taunt the Lord God. But each time, Jesus's response was, "It is written..." If the devil challenged Jesus about His Father's love, affirmation, and identity, then He certainly will challenge you. But God wants to secure your heart in these things—forever.

IN SUMMARY

A proper understanding of love, identity, and purpose is essential to the process of being set free. We have seen how Genesis 1:26-28 speaks to all three of those important aspects of life in Christ. I think of Romans 8:15-17 as the New Testament counterpart to the Genesis 1 passage. In it, God says He gave us the "Spirit of adoption," which brings us into intimacy with Him, and then He reveals His awesome love for us. Next, the Holy Spirit reveals that we are children of God. This establishes our true identity and allows us to say confidently, "I am now accepted into the family of God as His beloved child." Lastly, we are told that we are, "joint heirs with Christ," which reveals purpose as we join with Jesus to advance God's Kingdom and set the captives free.

♥ TAKE IT TO HEART

Have you struggled with any of these areas: *Love, Identity,* or *Purpose*? When you survey your life, do you see where you have believed lies about who you are, what God thinks about you, or His heart toward you and your purpose on this earth? Take some time to dialogue with God and ask Him to reveal any places where you need healing and a God-breathed perspective.

TAKE IT TO GOD

Dear Father God, I come in the name of Jesus and ask You to give me the Spirit of adoption, so that I might know Your love. I also ask You to give me a revelation of my identity as a child of God and as a joint heir with Jesus. Help me to fully experience Your love and acceptance. Lord, I thank You for the great salvation that You paid for at the Cross. Help me to walk in everything You have purchased for me. Now, give me strength to join You in Your ministry of setting the captives free, bringing life to those around me, and advancing Your Kingdom on earth as it is in Heaven. In Jesus's name, Amen.

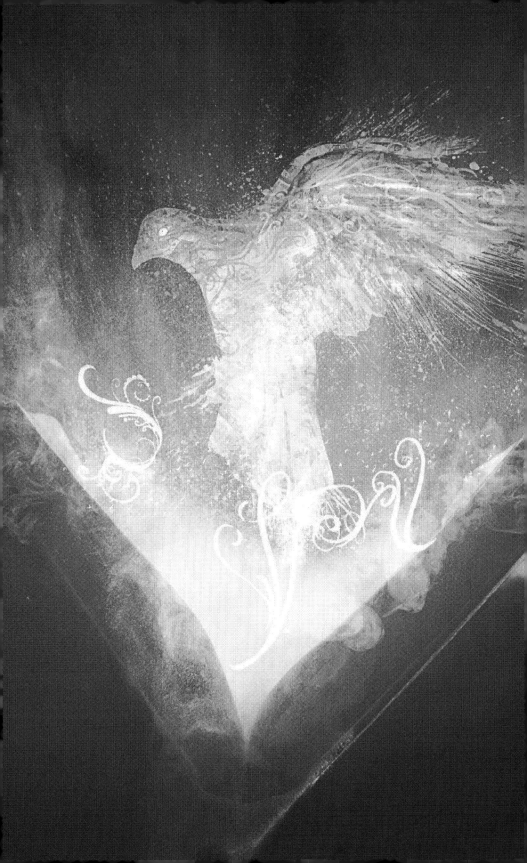

Receiving and Embracing the Holy Spirit

POWER OF FREEDOM

Perhaps you were raised in a Christian home, attended church all of your life, and tried to live by God-given principles, but were much like the disciples whom Paul met in Ephesus, who had never heard about the Holy Spirit (see Acts 19:1-7). Personally, after my experience of being baptized with the Holy Spirit, the reality of the Father's love and my true identity as a beloved son was powerfully clear.

After your salvation (being born again), receiving and embracing God as Spirit is vital and will empower you to walk in freedom. The baptism with the Holy Spirit, which was the "Promise of the Father" Jesus spoke of in Acts 1:4, is so much more than a onetime experience. If we are going to be the army of God and be disciples who minister (Luke 4:18, 19), we need the *power* of the Holy Spirit and His manifestations. Through the Scriptures presented in this chapter, you will see for yourself that the Holy Spirit is God, and that He has come to live in us and lead us into the abundant life that is available through Jesus.

Before His crucifixion, Jesus promised His disciples that the Holy Spirit, who would be just like He was, would come to them (John 14:16). The Holy Spirit did come at Pentecost (Acts 2:1-4) with power, anointing, and an affirmation of God's design for each one. It was a life-altering event for those in the Upper Room that day!

His assignment and His desires haven't changed over the 2,000 years since that encounter. He is still our Helper, Comforter, Counselor, Strengthener, Teacher, and Revealer of Truth. It's imperative that we understand and embrace the role of the

"If we are going to be the army of God... we need POWER."

Holy Spirit in our lives in order to grow and mature in God. If we do not develop our own personal intimacy with the Holy Spirit—allowing Him to reveal Jesus to us and really listening to what He says—we will never have true relationship with the Lord; we will only have religion. As we seek to minister healing and wholeness to others, we need an intimate relationship with the Holy Spirit so that, as He leads them to freedom, we can also follow Him.

Who is the Holy Spirit?

Simply stated, the Holy Spirit is God. He is also called the *Paraclete* and is the third person of the Trinity (Father, Son, and Holy Spirit). He is a divine Person with a mind, emotions, and a will. After Jesus's resurrection and brief visit before his ascension into Heaven, He said He would send the Holy Spirit...and He did. He sent the Holy Spirit to exercise a worldwide ministry, empowering believers to fulfill God's purposes on earth. Today, the Holy Spirit illuminates the minds of people, makes us yearn for God, and makes spiritual truth understandable to us. All over the world, the Holy Spirit is drawing men to Christ, and He lives in the hearts of believers, helping us each day. To be Spirit-filled Christians is to be the kind of Christians that God wants us to be.

It is so important for anyone who is serious about receiving the freedom and healing that is available from the Lord to put aside all reservations about the Holy Spirit and fully embrace Him.

Let's look at His role and function in our lives:

1. **He is God:**

   "God is Spirit, and those who worship Him must worship in spirit and truth." John 4:24

   "Now the Lord is the Spirit; and where the Spirit of the Lord is, there is liberty." 2 Corinthians 3:17

   "But when the Helper comes, whom I shall send to you from the Father, the Spirit of truth who proceeds from the Father, He will testify of Me." John 15:26

2. **He is our Helper:**

   "And I will pray the Father, and He will give you another Helper, that He may abide with you forever—the Spirit of truth, whom the world cannot receive, because it neither sees Him nor knows Him; but you know Him, for He dwells with you and will be in you." John 14:16, 17

   "Nevertheless, I tell you the truth. It is to your advantage that I go away; for if I do not go away, the Helper will not come to you; but if I depart, I will send Him to you."

   John 16:7

   Jesus said that the Father would send another Helper who would abide with us forever. This is the Holy Spirit. The word *another* means that He is just like Jesus. He is our Helper, Comforter, and Strengthener; He is *the Spirit of truth*. He promises that we will know Him, "for He dwells with [us] and will be in [us]" (John 14:17). In fact, Jesus told His disciples that it was actually good for them that He go away, so that they could receive and experience the Holy Spirit. (John 16:7)

3. He is our Teacher; The Spirit of Truth:

"But the Helper, the Holy Spirit, whom the Father will send in My name, He will teach you all things, and bring to your remembrance all things that I said to you" (John 14:26).

"I still have many things to say to you, but you cannot bear them now. However, when He, the Spirit of truth, has come, He will guide you into all truth; for He will not speak on His own authority, but whatever He hears He will speak; and He will tell you things to come. He will glorify Me, for He will take of what is Mine and declare it to you. All things that the Father has are Mine. Therefore, I said that He will take of Mine and declare it to you" (John 16:12-15).

"But as it is written: 'Eye has not seen, nor ear heard, nor have entered into the heart of man the things which God has prepared for those who love Him.' But God has revealed them to us through His Spirit. For the Spirit searches all things, yes, the deep things of God. For what man knows the things of a man except the spirit of the man which is in him? Even so, no one knows the things of God except the Spirit of God. Now we have received, not the spirit of the world, but the Spirit who is from God, that we might know the things that have been freely given to us by God. These things we also speak, not in words which man's wisdom teaches but which the Holy Spirit teaches, comparing spiritual things with spiritual. But the natural man does not receive the things of the Spirit of God, for they are foolishness to him; nor can he know them, because they are spiritually discerned." (1 Corinthians 2:9-14)

"But the anointing which you have received from Him abides in you, and you do not need that anyone teach you; but as the same anointing teaches you concerning all things, and is true, and is not a lie, and just as it has taught you, you will abide in Him." 1 John 2:27

4. He is the Spirit of Adoption:

"For you did not receive the spirit of bondage again to fear, but you received the Spirit of adoption by whom we cry out, 'Abba, Father.'" Romans 8:15

Through the experience of receiving the "adoption" by the Holy Spirit, we come to know and are secure in one of the most awesome aspects of the Christian life—truly, deeply, and personally receiving the love of the Father.

These Scriptures make it clear that the Holy Spirit's purpose and role in our lives is to be our Teacher and guide. He is the Spirit of truth and He leads us into truth—the truth that makes us free. He will speak to us, comfort us, tell us things to come, and glorify Jesus by taking what belongs to Him and declaring it to us. This is the anointing we have received from Him, the Holy Spirit, who abides in us.

The supernatural ministry of the Holy Spirit is fulfilled daily in our lives by:

- † Being endued with power from on high
- † Receiving power to be God's witness
- † Receiving power to overcome
- † Receiving the Spirit of adoption
- † Receiving comfort, help, and strength
- † Having Him lead us into truth
- † Having Him speak to us

Receiving the Holy Spirit

Before His crucifixion, Jesus told His disciples that it was to their advantage for Him to go away (John 16:7). Only after He was gone could the Holy Spirit come. What an interesting statement He made. He later told these same disciples not to leave Jerusalem until they were endued with the power of the Holy Spirit (Luke 24:49). This is the account of the *Great Commission*. He was sending them out into all the world to make disciples of all nations. He had breathed on them to receive the Holy Spirit (John 20:22), but they needed to be empowered!

We, too, must fully receive and embrace the Holy Spirit and His power if we are going to be effective disciples, who make a difference and advance the Kingdom of God on earth. We all need the power of God to walk through this life. People who have been wounded or caught in the snares of the enemy need freedom and the power to fulfill their purpose. In this world, we will have tribulation: challenges, pain, and difficulties. Even so, God has made a way for us to overcome through the power of His Holy Spirit. Through a deep and intimate relationship with God the Holy Spirit, we will be able to hear His voice clearly, follow His leading, be convicted of sin, know truth, be His witness, receive comfort, and be empowered to do all that God has planned for us.

"The Spirit of the Lord is upon Me, because He has anointed Me to preach the gospel to the poor; He has sent Me to heal the brokenhearted, to proclaim liberty to the captives and recovery of sight to the blind, to set at liberty those who are oppressed; to proclaim the acceptable year of the Lord." Luke 4:18-19

John the Baptist told us, "He [Jesus] will baptize you with the Holy Spiritandfire"(Matthew3:11).Though some theological persuasions might not agree, it is clear that Jesus felt it was necessary for His disciples to receive the power of the Holy Spirit before they entered their next phase of ministry (Acts 1:4-8). In fact, Jesus Himself did not begin His ministry until He had received the Holy Spirit in a way that was visible to others (Luke 3:22; 4:14). He received the Holy Spirit, was anointed by the Holy Spirit, and ministered in the power of the Holy Spirit.

> "And the Holy Spirit descended in bodily form like a dove upon Him, and a voice came from heaven which said, 'You are My beloved Son; in You I am well pleased.'" Luke 3:22

> "The Spirit of the Lord is upon Me, because He has anointed Me to preach the gospel to the poor; He has sent Me to heal the brokenhearted, to proclaim liberty to the captives and recovery of sight to the blind, to set at liberty those who are oppressed; to proclaim the acceptable year of the Lord."
> Luke 4:18-19

> "God anointed Jesus of Nazareth with the Holy Spirit and with power, who went about doing good and healing all who were oppressed by the devil, for God was with Him."
> Acts 10:38

The Baptism of the Holy Spirit

From the beginning of the church and throughout history, the baptism of the Holy Spirit has been an integral and crucial aspect of the lives of God's people. This baptism has been experienced by millions of people worldwide, and it is intended for us today. Receiving the baptism of the Holy Spirit is extremely important if we are going to advance the Kingdom of God on earth.

Let's look at what Scripture has to say about being baptized with the Holy Spirit:

> "But you shall receive power when the Holy Spirit has come upon you; and you shall be witnesses to Me in Jerusalem, and in all Judea and Samaria, and to the end of the earth." Acts 1:8

> "Behold, I send the Promise of My Father upon you; but tarry in the city of Jerusalem until you are endued with power from on high." Luke 24:49

> "When the Day of Pentecost had fully come, they were all with one accord in one place. And suddenly there came a sound from Heaven, as of a rushing mighty wind, and it filled the whole house where they were sitting. Then there appeared to them divided tongues, as of fire, and one sat on each of them. And they were all filled with the Holy Spirit and began to speak with other tongues, as the Spirit gave them utterance." Acts 2:1-4

> "While Peter was still speaking these words, the Holy Spirit fell upon all those who heard the word. And those of the circumcision who believed were astonished, as many as came with Peter, because the gift of the Holy Spirit had been poured out on the Gentiles also. For they heard them speak with tongues and magnify God. Then Peter answered, 'Can anyone forbid water, that these should not be baptized who have received the Holy Spirit just as we have?' And he commanded them to be baptized in the name of the Lord. Then they asked him to stay a few days." Acts 10:44-48

> "And it happened, while Apollos was at Corinth, that Paul, having passed through the upper regions, came to Ephesus. And finding some disciples he said to them, 'Did you receive the Holy Spirit when you believed?' So, they said to

him, 'We have not so much as heard whether there is a Holy Spirit.' And he said to them, 'Into what then were you baptized?' So, they said, 'Into John's baptism.' Then Paul said, 'John indeed baptized with a baptism of repentance, saying to the people that they should believe on Him who would come after him, that is, on Christ Jesus.' When they heard this, they were baptized in the name of the Lord Jesus. And when Paul had laid hands on them, the Holy Spirit came upon them, and they spoke with tongues and prophesied." Acts 19:1-6

"Now when the apostles who were at Jerusalem heard that Samaria had received the word of God, they sent Peter and John to them, who, when they had come down, prayed for them that they might receive the Holy Spirit. For as yet He had fallen upon none of them. They had only been baptized in the name of the Lord Jesus. Then they laid hands on them, and they received the Holy Spirit..." Acts 8:14-24

Jesus promised that God would give us the Holy Spirit if we asked Him. But the enemy fights, with everything that he has, so that we will not receive the Holy Spirit. He does not want Christians to be empowered to do anything. Therefore, when we think about the Holy Spirit, the enemy tries to draw our attention to tongues or some other manifestation, so that we will miss this gift of truly receiving Him and being empowered by Him. We must receive the Holy Spirit and allow Him to empower us to do the work of ministry He has called us to do. If we are going to walk in the truth of God's freedom, we must be baptized with the Holy Spirit (sometimes called baptized *in* the Holy Spirit). A person who is baptized with the Holy Spirit is literally *immersed* in the Holy Spirit.

There are usually some outward manifestations of receiving the Holy Spirit, one of which is speaking in unknown tongues. Speaking in another tongue was normal in the experience of first century Christians but speaking in tongues is not the real issue. The important point is receiving power when the Holy Spirit has come upon you (Acts 1:8). Speaking in tongues is a benefit for the believer but receiving Him is the most important act.

God wants to answer your heart-cry for that sovereign, empowering presence in your life.

Have YOU received the Holy Spirit? He wants to answer your heart cry for that sovereign, empowering presence in your life.

IN SUMMARY

The Holy Spirit is God. He is our Helper, our Teacher, our Comforter, and our Friend. He is the Spirit of Truth and is the One who reveals the Word to us and leads us into truth. He is the Spirit of adoption and reveals the love of the Father to us. The Holy Spirit speaks to us what He hears from Heaven and reveals the things that have been freely given to us. He is the key to every aspect of an intimate, vibrant, fulfilling relationship with God and the door to effective ministry. All we need to do is ask, receive, and fully embrace the gift of the Holy Spirit (Luke 11:9-13).

♥   TAKE IT TO HEART

Have you had beliefs or questions about the role of the Holy Spirit in your life? As you've read through this chapter, has God highlighted anything to you that needs to be answered? What is your heart saying about your desire to walk in power and victory, truth and understanding? The Lord wants to bring all the fullness of His presence, His love, and His gifts into your life today. Ask Him—He will answer!

☖ TAKE IT TO GOD

Dear God, forgive me for not recognizing or receiving You as the Spirit. I ask that You baptize me now with the Holy Spirit and with fire, so that Your supernatural power can flow through me. I surrender control of my life to You and give You a place in my heart and life. I invite You to empower me to be Your witness. I receive Your Holy Spirit and all of Your manifestations and gifts, that I might walk in Your purposes, anointing, and glory. In Jesus's name, Amen.

The Battleground

STANDING FOR FREEDOM

The thief does not come except to steal, and to kill, and to destroy. I have come that they may have life, and that they may have it more abundantly. John 10:10

Many people do not even realize there is a very real battle taking place in the spiritual realm. We are not living in a time of peace but in a time of war. Sure, it may not feel like you are in the heat of battle, but there is a war raging in the spiritual realm, in the heavenly places, that is as fierce and as real as any battle here on earth. And what happens in the spiritual realm has influence over the physical realm.

It's a war that is raging between God's children and the forces of darkness. It is led by the devil, and earth is the battlefield. The devil and a third of the angels were kicked out of Heaven (Revelation 12:4, 7-9) and there has been conflict in the heavenlies ever since. Ultimately, satan will be cast into the lake of fire, along with his demons, when Jesus returns at the end of time (Revelation 20:10). Until then, the Kingdom of God remains at war with the kingdom of darkness (Matthew 13:36-43).

"So the Lord God said to the serpent: 'Because you have done this, you are cursed more than all cattle, And more than every beast of the field; On your belly you shall go, And you shall eat dust all the days of your life. And I will put enmity between you and the woman, and between your seed and her Seed; He shall bruise your head, And you shall bruise His heel.'" Genesis 3:14-15

In this war, we do not battle against other people (flesh and blood), but against the forces of darkness, principalities, and powers in *epouranios* (the heavenly realm). Jesus dealt with the devil in the wilderness (Luke 4:1-11) and continued to cast out demons when He encountered them. We, too, battle against the devil and his demonic hosts, but God has given us ALL power and authority over the enemy. We are in this conflict and we must fight! The Good News, however, is that Jesus has already defeated the devil and we can experience His victory in our lives. God wants to use us as a proclamation to the heavenly realm, through which He will demonstrate and proclaim to all of earth, Heaven, and hell that there is a God and the LORD, He is God!

"God wants to use YOU as a proclamation to the heavenly realm."

The Bible gives us the following instructions so that we can fight well against our true enemies, knowing Jesus has secured the victory for us and defeated the devil. We fight from a place of victory—His victory for us!

> "Finally, my brethren, be strong in the Lord and in the power of His might. Put on the whole armor of God, that you may be able to stand against the wiles of the devil. For we do not wrestle against flesh and blood, but against principalities, against powers, against the rulers of the darkness of this age, against spiritual hosts of wickedness in the heavenly places." Ephesians 6:10-12

> "Be sober, be vigilant; because your adversary the devil walks about like a roaring lion, seeking whom he may devour. Resist

him, steadfast in the faith, knowing that the same sufferings are experienced by your brotherhood in the world."

1 Peter 5:8-9

"Having disarmed principalities and powers, He made a public spectacle of them, triumphing over them in it."

Colossians 2:15

"He who sins is of the devil, for the devil has sinned from the beginning. For this purpose, the Son of God was manifested, that He might destroy the works of the devil." 1 John 3:8

"...What is the exceeding greatness of His power toward us who believe, according to the working of His mighty power which He worked in Christ when He raised Him from the dead and seated Him at His right hand in the heavenly places, far above all principality and power and might and dominion, and every name that is named, not only in this age but also in that which is to come. And He put all things under His feet and gave Him to be head over all things to the church, which is His body, the fullness of Him who fills all in all." Ephesians 1:19-23

Our Authority in Christ

God has always had all authority. It was man who lost his authority and favored position with God in the Garden of Eden. Jesus came to earth as a man to reclaim for humanity the authority that man had lost. He did this at the Cross. Now, through faith in Jesus and what He did at the cross, we have been restored to this favorable position of relationship with God and have been given authority over the evil one and authority to advance the Kingdom of God. Because we are *in Christ*, we have the same authority that Jesus has.

We have been given *power* to accomplish all that the Father has given us to do. And greater still, we have also been given *authority* in Christ to execute that power. These two important words in Greek are as follows:

† **AUTHORITY** = *Exousia*

Definition: power to act, authority, 1) power, authority, weight, especially: moral authority, influence, 2) in a quasi-personal sense, derived from later Judaism, of a spiritual power, and hence of an earthly power. (Strong's 1849)

† **POWER** = *Dunamis*

Definition: strength power, ability, 1) inherent power, power residing in a thing by virtue of its nature, or which a person or thing exerts and puts forth, 2) power for performing miracles, 3) moral power and excellence of soul. (Strong's 1411)

"And Jesus came and spoke to them, saying, 'All authority has been given to Me in Heaven and on earth. Go therefore and make disciples of all nations, baptizing them in the name of the Father and of the Son and of the Holy Spirit, teaching them to observe all things that I have commanded you; and lo, I am with you always, even to the end of the age. Amen.'" Matthew 28:18-20

"Then the seventy returned with joy, saying, 'Lord, even the demons are subject to us in Your name.' And He said to them, 'I saw Satan fall like lightning from Heaven. Behold, I give you the authority to trample on serpents and scorpions, and over all the power of the enemy, and nothing shall by any means hurt you. Nevertheless do not rejoice in this, that the spirits are subject to you, but rather rejoice because your names are written in Heaven.'" Luke 10:17-20

"Then I heard a loud voice saying in Heaven, 'Now salvation, and strength, and the kingdom of our God, and the power of His Christ have come, for the accuser of our brethren, who accused them before our God day and night, has been cast down. And they overcame him by the blood of the Lamb and by the word of their testimony, and they did not love their lives to the death." Revelation 12:10-11

"But if I cast out demons by the Spirit of God, surely the kingdom of God has come upon you." Matthew 12:28

Pathways of Access

There are many avenues and methods through which the enemy gains access into our lives, as we will discuss in later chapters. But two very important areas need to be brought to light here: _Intrusion_ and _Legal Ground_.

"Are you aware that every thought you have may not originate in your own mind?"

Intrusion happens when the devil trespasses and tries to get us to believe a lie, thereby deceiving us in some way. Demons are always looking for an opportunity to harass and afflict people; if we do not resist the devil and his demons, they will do exactly that. The devil intrudes in two very important areas—our thoughts and our relationships.

We do not believe that Christians can be possessed, but we can certainly be oppressed and afflicted by evil spirits if we do not understand Jesus's victory and our position of victory in Him. Even if we do understand this, the enemy can still try to afflict us. We must stand against him because he roams about "seeking whom he may devour" (1 Peter 5:8).

The first battle that we face is the one that takes place in our mind and is waged over our thoughts. Are you aware that every thought you have may not originate in your own mind? The devil is the father of lies (John 8:44); he is the accuser of the brethren and he tries to deceive us (Revelation 12:9-10). He constantly bombards our minds with lies and improper thoughts. These are the "fiery darts" that our shield of faith can deflect (Ephesians 6:16).

In this way, the devil tries to gain access into our lives. If we believe him and his lies, we end up in bondage. If we believe the truth, the truth will make us free. That is the reason we must learn to take every thought captive to the obedience of God (2 Corinthians 10:3-5). If we do not take thoughts captive and win this battle in the mind, we will soon find that we have opened the door for the devil to afflict us even more.

The second area in which we see intrusion operating is within our relationships. The enemy is always trying to get us upset and angry with people—especially those closest to us. Is there anyone who doesn't struggle at times with relationships? How often do we find ourselves upset, frustrated, and struggling in a relationship because of something a person said or did? If we do not take our thoughts captive, we will become angry, bitter, and may even move into sin (Ephesians 4:26-27). Regardless of his scheme or how it's presented, the devil is always trying to gain access to us in some way.

Legal Ground is exactly what you might think it is. It is a legal right to access or possess. When we sin, we actually give permission to the devil and his demons to come and harass us. We are *allowing* them entry into our lives—giving them legal access to us. Let's look at the story of Cain and Abel in Genesis 4:1-8 to get a better understanding of *open doors*.

Cain brought an offering to God that he knew was unacceptable, and Cain got really angry. In the following verse, God says, "If you do well, will you not be accepted? And if you do not do well, sin lies at the door. And its desire is for you, but you should rule over it" (Genesis 4:7).

It is clear from this Scripture that sin is personified, and the enemy had legal access to Cain because of sin and the choices and decisions which he made. We, like Cain, have made choices and decisions that have had serious consequences. But God says we can choose to do what is right and we must rule over sin. Paul explains further in this verse:

> "Do you not know that to whom you present yourselves slaves to obey, you are that one's slaves whom you obey, whether of sin leading to death, or of obedience leading to righteousness?" Romans 6:16

Understanding the significance of legal ground is extremely important when trying to be free. We must determine where and how we have given the enemy legal entrance into our lives and then learn how to regain that ground and take back the territory. As you continue in your study of *Free Indeed*, you will be given more insight and information so that you can look deeper into these areas of strongholds and trauma, inner vows, sin, and open doors. God's heart for you is that you be completely FREE to live an abundant life of peace, joy, and purpose as His beloved child.

IN SUMMARY

We are not at war with other people, although it often seems that way. The Word is clear that we battle against the forces of darkness and wickedness in the heavenly places. The struggles we face, the challenges, the pain, and brokenness are brought on by an enemy who wants only to kill, steal, and destroy.

But God has given us, through Jesus Christ, all authority, power, love, and a sound mind to wage war against this foe. We have only to step into our place and position as God's children, take up the full armor of God, and fight, knowing that the battle has already been won.

We can tear down principalities and powers, command the enemy to flee, close legal doors of invasion, and stop all harassment and intrusion in the mighty, powerful name of Jesus. We take back all that is rightfully ours, and confidently proclaim the Kingdom of God has come!

♥ TAKE IT TO HEART

Have you considered that you may have opened the door to the devil and given him legal rights in some areas of your life? Perhaps you did not even realize what was taking place—the choices and decisions that could give access to the enemy. Take a few moments and talk with God about this. Ask His Holy Spirit to convict you of any sin and to reveal those places of intrusion.

A very real war is being waged in the heavenlies for your life and the lives of those you love. You may need repentance, deliverance, ministry, and healing in those areas. This is a battle that secured an eternal victory, through the life of Jesus, paid for at the Cross. And He wants to give YOU that same authority to stand against the power of the enemy and the forces of darkness. Would you pray now?

TAKE IT TO GOD

Dear God, I repent and ask Your forgiveness for my sins, my disobedience, my stubbornness, and for making decisions and choices that have given access to the enemy and the kingdom of darkness. I have suffered and lost Your blessings, I know. I renounce the enemy. I take authority, in the name of Jesus, over every area the devil has invaded, and I take back the legal ground and close the door to all intrusion. Please release me from all my guilt and shame. I ask that You, Lord, fill me afresh with power to walk in the authority you have given to me. I receive the fullness of Your healing and love. In Jesus's name, Amen.

Unlocking Important Truths

KEYS TO FREEDOM

"If My people who are called by My name will humble themselves, and pray and seek My face, and turn from their wicked ways, then I will hear from heaven, and will forgive their sin and heal their land." 2 Chronicles 7:14

The heart of God is to see the body of Christ educated, equipped, and empowered to live free and stay free—to be whole, restored, transformed, and ready to impact our world with a message of hope. We have been given principles and keys in the Word to unlock truths and align our heart attitudes to the heart of the Father. Let's look at some of these important truths to help enable us to walk in freedom.

1. Humble yourself before God

When we humble ourselves, we are acknowledging that we need the Lord not only for help, but for life itself. If we humble ourselves, then the Lord can release grace in our lives. A lack of humility before the Lord is one of the biggest obstacles to receiving from Him. If we do not humble ourselves, God's grace will not be released. Humility is not just acting in a certain self-effacing way, but a heart attitude of being totally dependent upon God. We must have God's grace and His unmerited favor in our lives. In order to receive it, we must humble ourselves before Him.

Jesus is our example of humility. In Matthew 11:29, He says, "Take My yoke upon you and learn from Me, for I am gentle and lowly in heart, and you will find rest for your souls."

James 4:6b is very clear: "God resists the proud but gives grace to the humble."

If we do not humble ourselves, we stay in our pride and God actually resists us. If you do not seem to have the grace you need in your life, recognize that you may be having a problem with pride. Pride can manifest in various ways. An unwillingness to learn, thinking you're better than others,

"A lack of favor and grace in your life may be an indication of pride."

wanting constant attention, criticizing and judging others, or refusing to ask for help. But there is a solution and the answer is found in prayer and humility. We can make the choice, as an act of our will, to obey God's Word. Humble yourself, repent, and receive God's forgiveness and grace. It is freely yours.

> "Humble yourselves in the sight of the Lord, and He will lift you up." James 4:10

> "Likewise, you younger people, submit yourselves to your elders. Yes, all of you be submissive to one another, and be clothed with humility, for 'God resists the proud, but gives grace to the humble.' Therefore, humble yourselves under the mighty hand of God, that He may exalt you in due time."
>
> 1 Peter 5:5-6

2. Seek God, not the things of God

> "But from there you will seek the Lord your God, and you will find Him if you seek Him with all your heart and with all your soul." Deuteronomy 4:29

This is a serious issue of priority and incredibly important. God loves us and His heart is for us. He is a God of abundance and has not withheld anything from us. His love and heart are clearly revealed through Jesus's example as He went about doing good, healing the sick, and bringing deliverance. It's critical that we forever settle the issue about the goodness of God. He declares that He has good things in store for us. In the Old Testament, the children of Israel continually said, "Oh, give thanks to the Lord, for He is good! For His mercy endures forever" (Psalm 106:1). This is God's true nature as revealed in His Word.

> "Now the Lord descended in the cloud and stood with him there and proclaimed the name of the Lord. And the Lord passed before him and proclaimed, 'The Lord, the Lord God, merciful and gracious, longsuffering, and abounding in goodness and truth.'" Exodus 34:5-6

He is a jealous God, however, and He zealously wants all of our affection and attention. His desire is that we would seek Him—not just His hand (the things He will give us). The truth is that making anything or anyone more important to us than God is a form of idolatry. When the Israelites turned their hearts from God, idolatry led to their downfall.

"If we seek Him with our whole heart, we will find Him...and discover everything we need."

God has not changed. He still wants our whole heart. Jesus said that God's greatest commandment is to love Him "with all your heart" (Matthew 22:37). He wants us to love Him with all of our heart, not just to seek Him for relief from our pain, for the provision He brings, or the blessings He gives. If we seek Him with our whole heart, we will find Him (Jeremiah 29:13); when we find Him, then we discover everything we need. "Seek Me and live" (Amos 5:4).

"For I know the thoughts that I think toward you, says the Lord, thoughts of peace and not of evil, to give you a future and a hope. Then you will call upon Me and go and pray to Me, and I will listen to you. And you will seek Me and find Me, when you search for Me with all your heart. I will be found by you, says the Lord." Jeremiah 29:11-14a

"But seek first the Kingdom of God and His righteousness, and all these things shall be added unto you." Matthew 6:33

Prayer

Perhaps take a moment to reflect upon what you've just read and pray: *"Father, please forgive me for seeking Your hand and not Your face. Forgive me for idolatry, for not loving You first with all of my heart. I repent of all pride and I humble myself under Your mighty, loving hand. I ask You to release Your grace in my life as You conform me to Your image. Amen.*

3.   Take responsibility for your actions and responses

"Whoever conceals his transgressions will not prosper, but he who confesses and forsakes them will obtain mercy." Proverbs 28:13 (ESV)

"Therefore, brothers, be all the more diligent to confirm your calling and election sure, for if you practice these qualities you will never fall." 2 Peter 1:10 (ESV)

To begin, we must call sin what God calls sin and repent. Many times, our problems do not arise from what was done to us, but from our wrong responses to those things. When the fall took place in the Garden of Eden, Adam and Eve both blamed someone else for their actions (Genesis 3:11-13). This is often our attitude, as well. We want to blame others and not be held accountable for our thoughts and behaviors. We must, however, learn to take personal responsibility for our actions and attitudes. *Response - ability* means we have the ability to respond maturely and appropriately in situations.

Remember, "the wages of sin is death," separation from God (Romans 6:23). Jesus came to forgive our sins and, through the power of the Cross, He rendered sin powerless in our lives. We are no longer held captive to sin, but our *responsibility* is to turn from all sin (repent) and agree with God that sin is so horrible, it cost Jesus His life. Most people handle sin in one of these ways:

† Deny their actions, attitudes, and responses are sin by calling them "problems"

† Blame someone else

† Completely ignore what is going on

† Call sin what God calls sin (right response)

In which one of these various ways do you handle your sin? Do you see your actions, thoughts, and attitudes as sin and worthy of Jesus's death? If you do, and you accept personal responsibility for them, confess them, and truly turn from them. Not only will you be forgiven and cleansed, but you will also be given the power to overcome. Repentance is crucial because it releases the power of God in our lives.

It is essential to agree with God and identify any actions, attitudes, and responses that do not line up with Scripture as sin. In order to respond biblically to sin, we must confess and repent. It's necessary to do both.

† First, confess and agree with God. This is humility.
   Be honest as you tell Him how you have sinned
   (remember, He already knows).

† Second, repent (change the way you think, act, and respond).
   The Bible places major emphasis upon repentance.
   The sincerity of your repentance impacts your freedom.

"If we confess our sins, He is faithful and just to forgive us
our sins and to cleanse us from all unrighteousness."

1 John 1:9

"Confess your trespasses to one another, and pray for one
another, that you may be healed. The effective, fervent
prayer of a righteous man avails much." James 5:16

"He who covers his sins will not prosper, but whoever confesses and forsakes them will have mercy." Proverbs 28:13

4. Make a Choice to Forgive

Forgiveness (extending love and mercy to those who hurt you) is a
major key to freedom and the basis for walking in freedom. As we
go through *Free Indeed*, we will be forgiving those who have hurt
and wronged us, while asking for forgiveness for our own sins (1
John 1:9).

The freedom you experience will be determined by the depth of your
choice to forgive, which is *Love in Action*. John 13:34-35 tells us to,
"love one another; as I have loved you."

In this verse, we see Jesus's thoughts about the importance of forgiveness as He prays to the Father in the Lord's Prayer: "And forgive
us our debts, as we forgive our debtors." Matthew 6:12

Forgiveness has several different aspects that need to be considered. The following Scriptures give insight about how the Lord would have us forgive, what to do if we have been the offender (seek forgiveness), how much forgiveness is required of us, and how much the Lord desires to forgive.

"For if you forgive men their trespasses, your heavenly Father will also forgive you. But if you do not forgive men their trespasses, neither will your Father forgive your trespasses." Matthew 6:14-15

"Therefore if you bring your gift to the altar, and there remember that your brother has something against you, leave your gift there before the altar, and go your way. First be reconciled to your brother, and then come and offer your gift..." Matthew 5:23-24

"Get rid of all bitterness, rage and anger, brawling and slander, along with every form of malice. Be kind and compassionate to one another, forgiving each other, just as in Christ God forgave you." Ephesians 4:31-32 (NIV)

"Bear with each other and forgive one another if any of you has a grievance against someone. Forgive as the Lord forgave you." Colossians 3:13 (NIV)

Please take time to read a very powerful story about forgiveness found in Matthew 18:21-35.

Forgiveness is a choice, not a feeling. You forgive with your will, not with your emotions. If you have been hurt, neglected, or abused, you probably do not feel like you have the emotional strength to forgive. You may want revenge. It's human nature to want those who have hurt us to experience the pain, in some measure, that they have caused us. But this is not God's way. If we do not forgive, we literally *attach* or bind ourselves to that person or the people who hurt us. The result is that the pain and brokenness continue. But when you forgive and release, you will free yourself from the chains and allow God to work in the life of the one(s) who hurt you. The people who hurt us are usually people who are experiencing their own personal pain. The ability to see and understand that hurting people hurt people can help you forgive them.

Getting angry and harboring unforgiveness will throw open the door to torment and demonic activity in your life (Ephesians 4:26-27; Matthew 18:34-35). You can only close that door by extending forgiveness from the heart and allowing God to bring justice to the situation. You cannot change what happened to you, but you can determine how it affects you. You can forgive the person(s) who hurt you, receive healing and experience real freedom, or you can hold on to unforgiveness and allow bitterness to keep you in bondage. The choice is yours. Forgiving someone does not mean that you agree with what they have done.

> *"You cannot change what happened to you, but you can determine how it affects you."*

In order for your forgiveness to be real and from the heart, you may have to deal with your feelings and process through some of the pain, but the freedom that will come from forgiving will be worth the struggle of confronting, confessing, and releasing the trauma, pain, and anger.

It's important to recognize that Jesus forgave us a debt we could not pay. And you can only forgive because Christ has already forgiven you. Forgiveness is one of the greatest manifestations of love. It is the law of the Spirit in Christ Jesus that frees us from the law of sin and death (Romans 8:2). He forgave first (1 John 4:10). By His Spirit indwelling you, He gives you the power to forgive! This is following Jesus's example. Therefore, we must forgive those who have hurt us. By His grace, you are choosing to extend love and mercy instead of judgment.

Remember, "Love never fails!" 1 Corinthians 13:8

One final note—forgiving *ourselves* can sometimes be the hardest person to forgive, but it is imperative that you forgive yourself and not hold judgment, guilt, regret, and shame in your own heart. Jesus forgave YOU, and you need to forgive and release yourself.

"Forgiveness is one of the greatest manifestations of love."

IN SUMMARY

One of the most difficult challenges in our journey to freedom in this Christian walk is deciding and choosing to forgive others and ourselves. But on the other side of *choosing forgiveness* is the kind of life God intended for you when He sent His Son to die for your sins. It comes packaged with the freedom to bless others, to walk unhindered by bitterness and resentment, to relate confidently with God and people around you, and, most importantly, to be a living, walking display of the gospel and grace of Christ to a hurting world.

The Father has made a way through Jesus Christ, not only for us to be forgiven, but for us to be able to forgive others. He even empowers us to do so because He knows that therein lies our true freedom. It awaits you! Ask Him and draw near to God; in His love, you will find everything you need.

Dedicate some time for this process of walking through forgiving those who have caused you pain. As you pray and wait upon the Holy Spirit, He will reveal the people He wants you to forgive. This may require more time than you have right now, but you can start with the first person He brings to mind. Remember that this is a choice—a decision of your will. Feelings will come later. The following prayer will help direct you in the important steps to releasing and breaking free from the results and consequences of unforgiveness in your life. Know this:

"Whom the Son sets free is FREE INDEED!"

    TAKE IT TO GOD

Dear God, I thank You for Your love and extending grace, mercy, and forgiveness to me. I confess and repent for not extending the same to others who have hurt and rejected me. I give You my pain, rejection, trauma, and brokenness. I repent of all the anger I have held toward (name). Lord, I choose, in obedience to Your Word, to forgive and release (name) for (the offenses). I receive Your healing and freedom in my life. In Jesus's name, Amen.

As you prayed to forgive and release, we know that there were probably others whom God brought to mind. As you have time, take this sample prayer and insert the names of every person the Lord highlights for you. This is your opportunity to be released from any residual reminders of people or events which have caused pain. You'll experience great peace and healing as the Lord brings comfort and forgiveness to your heart.

In Matthew 5:44, Jesus said, "But I say to you, love your enemies, bless those who curse you, do good to those who hate you, and pray for those who spitefully use you and persecute you."

This passage in Matthew has four key components that are very important for walking in freedom. Although it might be hard to do at first, ask God to help you to step into a new perspective and view of what it means to "love one another as Christ has loved us" (John 13:34). May the JOY of the Lord be your strength!

1. **Love your enemies by forgiving them, which is extending love.**

2. **Bless those who have hurt you by speaking words of life and blessing.**

3. **Do good to those who hate you and find ways to demonstrate love.**

4. **Pray for those who hurt you, spitefully use you and cause pain.**

Generational Patterns

DOORS TO FREEDOM

Generational sins or patterns are the sins and actions committed by our forefathers that have been passed down to us through our families, becoming patterns that resulted from those sins. Just as we have certain DNA that carry sickness, diseases, or pre-dispositions for physical issues and appearance, we can also carry spiritual DNA from our ancestors. We inherit many of the negative tendencies or problems we could think of as curses. The Hebrew word for *iniquity* means, "a bent toward rebellion, perversity, or moral evil." (Ah.W.H, Strong's #5753, #5771). Iniquity is more than one act of sin or missing the mark. It is a system of sinful behavior, ignorance, or rebellion as a way of life.

Exodus 20:1-6 reveals this malady: "And God spoke all these words, saying: 'I am the Lord your God, who brought you out of the land of Egypt, out of the house of bondage. You shall have no other gods before Me. You shall not make for yourself a carved image—any likeness of anything that is in heaven above, or that is in the earth beneath, or that is in the water under the earth; you shall not bow down to them nor serve them. For I, the Lord your God, am a jealous God, visiting the iniquity of the fathers upon the children to the third and fourth generations of those who hate Me, but showing mercy to thousands, to those who love Me and keep My commandments.'"

Just looking back at your own family line to the fourth generation, you would find about thirty people who would be considered *ancestors*.

We don't fully understand all the ways in which we are connected to our parents, grandparents, and great-grandparents. But we do understand that someone's unique eye color, red hair, jawline, etc., can all be traced back through the family lineage.

All through the Old Testament, God reveals Himself as the God of Abraham, Isaac, and Jacob. The generations are important and, whether we like it or not, we are connected to our parents and our other ancestors. Many times, we make sinful or bad decisions that perpetuate the curses which have come down through the line. This is what we want to investigate in this chapter.

Indications of a Generational Pattern

When we use the word *pattern*, what we mean is that we are predisposed to making certain types of decisions or being more easily swayed in our areas of weakness. In the Bible, these are called curses. If there is a pattern of recurring sin or repeated problems in your life or in your family's lives, then there could be a curse operating (Deuteronomy 28:15-68). The following problems or tendencies could indicate that a curse is working in your life or in your family. Not everything is a curse, but if there are reoccurring situations throughout your family, it is probable that there is a curse that is operating.

 † Mental or emotional breakdown (Deuteronomy 28:28)

 † Chronic sickness, diseases, hereditary health issues (Deut. 28:22, 27, 35, 59)

 † Reproductive problems; miscarriage (Deut. 28:18)

 † Marital and Family problems; Divorce (Deut. 28:30,41; Proverbs 3:33; Malachi 2:14)

† Financial problems, not tithing (Malachi 3:8-10; Deut. 28:17, 29, 47, 48)

† Suicide, unnatural, premature deaths (Deut.28:26, 45, 53)

† Being accident prone, failures (Deut. 28:29)

† Uncontrolled anger, hate, unforgiveness (Matthew 5:22)

† Addictive behaviors (2 Corinthians 7:1)

"Christ has redeemed us from the curse of the law, having become a curse for us (for it is written, 'Cursed is everyone who hangs on a tree'), that the blessing of Abraham might come upon the Gentiles in Christ Jesus, that we might receive the promise of the Spirit through faith." Galatians 3:13-14

In this Scripture, we see that God has redeemed us from the curses being passed on from one generation to the next. This redemption comes as we understand that the root of our problems is in the spiritual realm. As we apply God's Word and power to our lives, and we choose to walk in righteousness and obedience to God, the chains of bondage will be broken. The freedom we have longed for can become reality!

Outlined below is a list of behaviors and activities that can open the door for curses. Prayerfully, before the Lord, read through this list and ask Him to reveal any family patterns that may be operating in your life. Then take time to follow the example in the **Prayer** to repent and renounce all sin, patterns, curses, or consequences in your life. Invite the Holy Spirit to release you and your family, and bring freedom, ending the access the enemy has had down through the generations.

Behaviors and Activities which Open Doors for Curses

- † Disobedience (Deuteronomy 28:15; Galatians 5:19-21)

- † Dishonoring parents (Exodus 20:12; Leviticus 20:9; Deuteronomy 5:16; Ephesians 6:1-3)

- † Rebelling against authority (Romans 13:1; Hebrews 13:17)

- † Anger and unforgiveness (Ephesians 4:26-27; Matthew 18:35)

- † Self-imposed curses; word curses and inner vows (Matthew 12:36-37)

- † Word curses spoken upon you by others (Numbers 22:6)

- † Involvement in the occult, witchcraft (Deuteronomy 19:9-14; Deut. 18:10-11)

- † Sexual sins such as adultery, fornication, illicit sex, homosexuality (Deut. 27:20-23)

- † Idolatry (Exodus 20:1-5)

- † Abortion and murder (Exodus 20:13)

- † Illegitimate birth (Deuteronomy 23:2-3)

- † Trusting in man (Jeremiah 17:5-8)

- † Stealing and lying (Zechariah 5:1-4)

- † Unscriptural covenants—Masonic, Occult, etc. (Exodus 23:32; 2 Corinthians 6:14)

- † Legalism (Galatians 3:10-14)

- † Not tithing (Malachi 3:8-10)

- † Anti-Semitism (Genesis 12:2-3)

PRAYER

Father God, I repent of the sins of my ancestors and of my sins in the area(s) of (list sins). I ask for Your forgiveness for all of these things. I renounce, rebuke, nullify, and cancel the curse of (specify curse). I declare that the curse, the assignment of the curse, and its effect is broken and canceled in my life from this day forward, in Jesus's name. I overcome by the blood of the Lamb, the word of my testimony. I believe by faith that Jesus took my curses upon Himself and now I ask You, Holy Spirit, to bring a release and freedom in my inner man. Now, satan, you no longer have access to me by these curses. In Jesus' name. Amen.

Justifying Sin Attitudes

Disobedience

This is not a subject or an area that we, as adults, normally spend much time considering. Yet, the Lord has a lot to say about this topic. Throughout the Bible, we see that all disobedience to God is called sin. It always gives legal ground to the enemy and is an open door to the devil and his demons. So, it's imperative that we close all open doors of disobedience and not allow the enemy access.

Galatians 5:19-21 lists many deeds of the flesh, and we are told that those who practice such things will not inherit the Kingdom of God:

> "Now the works of the flesh are evident, which are: adultery, fornication, uncleanness, lewdness, idolatry, sorcery, hatred, contentions, jealousies, outbursts of wrath, selfish ambitions, dissensions, heresies, envy, murders, drunkenness, revelries, and the like; of which I tell you beforehand, just as I also told

you in time past, that those who practice such things will not inherit the kingdom of God."

In this passage, the word for sorcery is actually *pharmakeia*, which is the root word for pharmacy or prescription drugs. It also means witchcraft. Those who practice, or repeatedly exercise, these things will not inherit the Kingdom of God. If you open the door to these areas of the flesh, you will soon find a demon working to stimulate these particular areas. The demon will then bring along other spirits to try to bring you into more bondage. Casting out demons or taking authority is important, but what is vital is that we make sure that all open doors are shut, and that we are filled with the Spirit and clothed in the armor of God (Ephesians 6:11-17).

Dishonor and Rebellion

These are two other areas that we do not typically or seriously consider as adults. We tend to relegate this area to children and teenagers. If you have a history of rebellion in your life, however, or have dishonored your parents, you may have given legal ground and access to the devil. Often, we see these two areas intertwined. This is such an important issue that it is the very first Commandment in the Bible which has a promise attached to it. Read what it says in Exodus 20:12 and is repeated by Peter in Ephesians:

> "Children, obey your parents in the Lord, for this is right. 'Honor your father and mother,' which is the first commandment with promise: 'that it may be well with you and you may live long on the earth.'" Ephesians 6:1-3

The Old Testament contextual definition of the Hebrew word *kabod*, or honor, means heavy or weighty. To honor someone is to give them weight in one's life, granting that person a position of respect and even authority. In the context of Exodus 20:12, it means to prize highly, care for, show respect for, and obey. Scripture affirms that NOT honoring our parents will cause problems for us. Honoring or not honoring our parents really sets the stage for the rest of our lives. If we have problems with our parents, we open the door to rebellion, and this rebellion opens the door for us to reject other forms of authority in our lives. The Bible is very clear about rebellion—rebellion is sin.

> "For rebellion is as the sin of witchcraft, and stubbornness is as iniquity and idolatry. Because you have rejected the word of the Lord, He also has rejected you from being king."
>
> 1 Samuel 15:23

Understanding Authority

Our response to authority often reveals an attitude of the heart. God has ordained authority as a place of many benefits and blessings, including safety, provision, success, care, nurturing and love, and He has established delegated authority in every sphere of life. It begins in the home with fathers and mothers, but also applies to church, work, school, and government. If we are not under authority, responding rightly (to God's delegated authority), then we are in rebellion. This opens the door to the enemy and keeps us from having any authority over him. Our authority is *in Christ* and not in ourselves. As we stay in relationship with Him, we have authority. Simply put, our authority comes from being submitted to the Lord and His delegated authority.

"Our response to authority often reveals an attitude of the heart that bears examination."

"Now when Jesus had entered Capernaum, a centurion came to Him, pleading with Him, saying, 'Lord, my servant is lying at home paralyzed, dreadfully tormented.' And Jesus said to him, 'I will come and heal him.' The centurion answered and said, 'Lord, I am not worthy that You should come under my roof. But only speak a word, and my servant will be healed. For I also am a man under authority, having soldiers under me. And I say to this one, 'Go' and he goes; and to another, 'Come,' and he comes; and to my servant, 'Do this,' and he does it.' When Jesus heard it, He marveled, and said to those who followed, 'Assuredly, I say to you, I have not found such great faith, not even in Israel!'" Matthew 8:5-10

The centurion understood the power of being under authority. He knew about it because he held a position of authority and had soldiers under him, submitted to his leadership. They obeyed him because he, as a military official, was under the authority of an even higher military official.

Matthew's account does not say whether or not the centurion knew whose authority Jesus was under, but he must have seen or heard how demons obeyed Jesus and that sicknesses left when Jesus spoke the *Word*. The centurion recognized this and said, "Only speak a word, and my servant will be healed." Matthew 5:8

The devil does not want us to understand authority, and he certainly does not want us to be under proper spiritual authority. Having a right relationship to authority really is an important issue for maturity, character, and commissioning in the Kingdom of God. We must allow the Holy Spirit to guide us, bring conviction, and enable us to fully embrace coming into alignment with Him in the area of submission to authority. If you are struggling with this question of authority, consider taking a few moments to draw away and pray the following prayer. Connect and align your heart to the Father's and experience a new level of healing.

PRAYER

"Father, I repent for my disobedience and any places of dishonoring my parents and ask You to forgive me; I understand this was rebellion. My sin has been against You, and I ask You to forgive me and cancel, by the shed blood of Jesus, any ground that the enemy has gained through this rebellion. Please show me where I have rejected and dishonored any authority you have placed in my life. I repent and ask You to forgive me and heal me from the effects of this sin and give me a true heart of submission. In Jesus's name, Amen."

Anger and Unforgiveness

While "anger" and "unforgiveness" are not necessarily considered sins, they can very easily lead to sinful behaviors. Anger is an emotion that needs to be handled properly and brought under control, if it is destructive. It can and will eventually lead to greater unforgiveness, bitterness and judgment and give legal ground to the devil and his demons. Paul understood the importance of dealing with anger quickly and appropriately, in order to close any open doors to the devil.

"Be angry, and do not sin": do not let the sun go down on your wrath, nor give place to the devil." Ephesians 4:26-27

In this verse, the Greek word for *give place* is a legal term that means *to give legal ground*. When we get angry and do not resolve our emotions properly, which is to forgive and let go, we open the door for the enemy to have legal access to us.

Unresolved anger is a real problem in many people's lives today. We see angry, frustrated, stressed, short-tempered people everywhere. The climate surrounding us in our cities, our government, and in our homes reflects the anger in hearts. The daily news is flooded with tragic stories of people whose anger has resulted in serious consequences and even death. The problem with unresolved anger is that it accumulates and escalates. Once a person allows an offense or anger to fester unresolved, then the next experience with a similar situation or issue, will just add to what was already there. Eventually, a person may explode by expressing their anger toward others. Or a person may implode and turn their anger inward, causing depression, physical problems or even suicide.

Anger often begins when we are very young—in the home—when we have problems and conflicts with our parents over any number of events or expectations. Regardless of what was said or done, whether it was right or wrong, any negative internal response to their words and/or actions can open the door to the enemy in our lives, especially if we have judged them or allowed a root of bitterness to take hold.

There are many reasons for anger. Some are justified and some not. Among others, we suffer because of unfulfilled expectations, injustices, abandonment, abuse, lies, disappointments, rejection, etc. But in every case, no matter what the cause, there is freedom granted us as we take personal responsibility for it. We must look truthfully at our anger, calling it sin, and repenting of each occurrence of anger and the consequences associated with it. The anecdote is prayer and forgiveness found in these verses:

> "But I say to you, love your enemies, bless those who curse you, do good to those who hate you, and pray for those who spitefully use you and persecute you." Matthew 5:44

> "For if you forgive men their trespasses, your heavenly Father will also forgive you. But if you do not forgive men their trespasses, neither will your Father forgive your trespasses." Matthew 6:14-15 (*The Lord's Prayer*)

Judgments and Inner Vows

These are often overlooked when we think about sin patterns. "Bitterroot Judgments" are judgments we make against someone or some institution, and those judgments lock us into negative patterns that are contrary to God. *Inner vows* are simply judg-

"Bitterroot judgments and inner vows can derail your destiny in God."

ments that we pronounce upon ourselves. This toxic combination will open the door of our lives to the enemy and lock us into beliefs, behaviors, and habit patterns that can derail our destiny, ruin us, and sabotage our efforts to succeed. Bitterroot judgments, along with unforgiveness, can devastate our lives and relationships. The Scriptures are clear about the seriousness of judgments. Instead, God's Word admonishes us to:

> "Pursue peace with all people, and holiness, without which no one will see the Lord: looking carefully lest anyone fall short of the grace of God; lest any root of bitterness springing up cause trouble, and by this many become defiled." Hebrews 12:14-15

> "'Judge not, that you be not judged. For with what judgment you judge, you will be judged; and with the measure you use, it will be measured back to you.'" Matthew 7:1-2

> "Therefore you are inexcusable, O man, whoever you are who judge, for in whatever you judge another you condemn yourself; for you who judge practice the same things. But we know that the judgment of God is according to truth against those who practice such things. And do you think this, O man, you who judge those practicing such things, and doing the same, that you will escape the judgment of God?" Romans 2:1-3

Inner vows are very destructive and set us into patterns that bring repeated failure, pain, and disappointment. They differ from bitterroot judgments because they are judgments that we rejection, pronounce against ourselves, our lives and others. Many times, we even speak these vows out loud without realizing that they bind us to curses and behaviors that we actually hate. We may have said things when we were young and then, having forgotten about them, wonder why they come back upon us later, fulfilling the judgments and vows. A few examples of these might be:

† "I will never be successful."

† "I will always be slow."

† "I will never treat my children the way my parents treated me."

† "I won't trust anyone ever again."

† "I will always be broke."

† "No one will ever want to marry me."

If you have made judgments or inner vows, you will either do the same thing, repeating that curse or you will do just the opposite, catapulting your life into performance and legalism.

These are just a few examples of what a person might say when making an inner vow. It's critical that you identify any vows or pronouncements you may have made. Look at your self-talk, thought patterns, and behaviors. Ask someone you trust if they have heard you speak negative, fatalistic, or judgmental things about yourself. Then ask the Father to reveal any inner vows you could have made in your life, knowingly or unknowingly. The Holy Spirit will faithfully lead you into all truth, bring conviction, and minister His love, forgiveness, and healing as you pray for a right heart and right perspective about who you REALLY are in Christ.

Soul Ties

This is a term we use to describe two *souls* being tied together. This may be a physical, mental, or emotional connection. While there is a place for healthy soul ties, as in a husband and wife, or parent and child, here we want to talk about *unhealthy* soul ties.

A soul tie is formed when your soul (mind, will, or emotions) become attached to someone in a way that creates dependency, obsession, fear, and anything else that would not be healthy. This can happen in family relationships between parents and children, in a dating relationship, in sports with a student and coach, and in religious settings with a pastor and a church member. One of the primary ways soul ties are formed is through ungodly sexual relations with someone who is not your spouse.

> "Now the body is not for sexual immorality but for the Lord, and the Lord for the body. And God both raised up the Lord and will also raise us up by His power. Do you not know that your bodies are members of Christ? Shall I then take the members of Christ and make them members of a harlot? Certainly not! Or do you not know that he who is joined to a harlot is one body with her? For 'the two,' He says, 'shall become one flesh.' But he who is joined to the Lord is one spirit with Him. Flee sexual immorality. Every sin that a man does is outside the body, but he who commits sexual immorality sins against his own body. Or do you not know that your body is the temple of the Holy Spirit who is in you, whom you have from God, and you are not your own? For you were bought at a price; therefore glorify God in your body and in your spirit, which are God's."
>
> 1 Corinthians 6:13-20

A soul tie can also be formed without actual sexual contact.

> "Do not be unequally yoked together with unbelievers. For what fellowship has righteousness with lawlessness...Or what part has a believer with an unbeliever...For you are the temple of the living God... 'Come out from among them and be separate, says the Lord...I will be a Father to you, and you shall be My sons and daughters, says the Lord Almighty.' Therefore, having these promises, beloved, let us cleanse ourselves... perfecting holiness in the fear of God."
>
> 2 Corinthians 6:14 - 7:1

Take some time to let the Holy Spirit show you if you have any unhealthy soul ties to anyone or ungodly connections that need to be broken. Then, repent and pray, asking the Lord to forgive you and bring wholeness to your soul. He will.

PRAYER

> *"Father, please show me every soul tie that I may have in my life and reveal any ungodly, unhealthy soul tie that may have me bound to any person, institution, or anything that is not of You. I repent of all sexual relations outside of marriage, which have opened the door for the enemy to have to access to me. Please sever any and all soul ties forever, canceling their power in my life. I receive Your healing and forgiveness. In Jesus's name, Amen"*

IN SUMMARY

Ancestral patterns or curses, learned behaviors, and generational sins can predispose us to making choices that breed brokenness and iniquity that seriously impact our lives. We find ourselves giving way to rebellion, bad decisions, patterns of immorality, addiction, negativity, and a myriad of other problems that hinder us from living a fulfilled life.

The enemy wants to keep us in bondage and in disobedience to God and His ways. But we must be willing to take an honest, courageous look at these sins, curses, and consequences to which we have given place. There is an answer in Christ Jesus, and there are doors to freedom being offered to you today. He will make a way where there seems to be none. It's His promise.

♥ TAKE IT TO HEART

You may have areas of brokenness and pain or repeated failure and addiction which have not been mentioned here. Your life and experiences are unique to you, but nonetheless under the mighty hand of a loving Father who wants to release you from any prison in which you have been. Take some dedicated time to read through the list in *Appendix D* and invite the Holy Spirit to reveal those areas of sin and weakness. In the prayer provided, follow through each of the open doors, breaking the power of that curse, and receiving God's full, complete healing and freedom.

🙏 TAKE IT TO GOD

Dear God, there are so many areas in my life that need Your healing hand. You came to set the captives free, and I have been held captive in sin, behaviors, and attitudes for too long. I repent and release them to You now and ask that You forgive me and keep me from returning to those destructive ways. Thank You for the grace that brought me to this place, seeking You and thanking You for the healing and freedom that's mine. In Jesus's name, Amen.

Ungodly Beliefs and Strongholds

Remember, John 8:31-32 says that if we know the truth, the truth will make us free. If the truth makes us free, then believing a lie will keep us in bondage. Most of the lies we believe are usually a result of unbelief (**incredulity** or skepticism especially in matters of religious faith – Merriam-Webster). And areas of unbelief are most likely *strongholds*.

Strongholds can be inherited or learned from our families and passed on through generations. They can also be formed through negative experiences or traumas in our lives.

2 Corinthians 10:3-5 says, "For though we walk in the flesh, we do not war according to the flesh. For the weapons of our warfare are not carnal but mighty in God for pulling down strongholds, casting down arguments and every high thing that exalts itself against the knowledge of God, bringing every thought into captivity to the obedience of Christ."

What does the Bible say about spiritual strongholds?

A **stronghold** is defined as "1. a place that has been fortified so as to protect it against attack; 2. a place where a particular cause or belief is strongly defended or upheld." Strongholds are designed to be a safe place (compellingtruth.org). As believers in Christ, we need to make the Lord our stronghold. He is our safe place and refuge (Psalm 27:1).

However, the strongholds we are talking about here are thought patterns (beliefs) that are contrary to the Word of God and brings us into defeat, which is most often characterized by hopelessness. If you believe that circumstances cannot and will never change, or that your past defines who you are, then you have a stronghold. Strongholds are supported by arguments and high things, and lofty opinions which are often rooted in pride and stand against the knowledge of God.

First, let's look at *arguments*. An argument is what satan uses against us as evidence to support the stronghold. Just like in a court of law, the prosecutor presents the evidence to support the claims against someone. Satan does the same thing to us. He uses past experiences, our circumstances, and situations as the evidence that we are doomed, without hope, and nothing can be remedied or fixed. He constantly reminds us that we have prayed and tried to see things change, but they have never changed. These arguments (so-called evidence) support the stronghold and keep us in bondage.

High things are the accusations against God. Satan hates God and tries to get us to believe lies about God. Satan tells us that God does not love us. If He really loved us, then why have all these bad things happened to us? He tells us that God is not good and that He is actually angry with us for our weaknesses and failures. He continues to bombard our minds with thoughts that God has abandoned or rejected us; God has favorites and will help some people but will not help us. The enemy's biggest lie is that God doesn't care about us or even hear our prayers.

Along with arguments, these accusations, which are high things against the knowledge of God, defend and support the stronghold. The enemy continues to attack our mind with negative thoughts—this is where the real battle is—so we must bring every thought into captivity to the obedience of God.

A great biblical example of this is found in Luke 3:21-22 and Luke 4:3-4. Jesus clearly shows us how to take thoughts captive and overcome the accusations of the enemy. In Luke 3:22, the Holy Spirit comes upon Jesus, and the Father speaks from Heaven, telling Jesus that He is His beloved Son and that He is well pleased with Him.

Forty days later, the devil challenges this Word from the Father by saying to Jesus, "If you are the Son of God..." (Luke 4:3). Jesus did not respond directly to the devil's innuendo, but said, "It is written, 'Man shall not live by bread alone, but by every word of God'" (Luke 4:4). Jesus took captive the thought that the devil tried to plant and responded according to the Word. He did not discuss or argue with the devil. He simply said, "It is written," and we must do the same when the enemy comes against us with thoughts and accusations.

What are some of the negative thoughts, strongholds, or ungodly beliefs which you carry? Perhaps you have believed lies about yourself, others, or God? Take some time to write them down and, as you do, pray for God to reveal things that are hidden. Here are some examples:

- † People in authority will always abuse me.

- † My life is so messed up, it can never be fixed.

- † My feelings don't count.

- † No one accepts me as I am.

- † I will always be alone.

- † I can never do enough to please God.

These are just a few of negative thought patterns, strongholds, or beliefs that people have. You may see something familiar to you in this list or have something totally different that you are allowing to shape who you are and what you believe. As you work through your list, ask the Lord for verses from His Word to counter and combat these negative thoughts.

What about the Issue of Shame?

A well-known and powerful ministry, *Restoring the Foundations* (RTF), estimates that over 50% of all Christians deal with a stronghold of *shame*. It's a powerful stronghold. Shame keeps us separated from God and from one another. In *Freedom from Your Past,* Ann Billington writes, "Guilt is a response to something you have done; it is a reaction to your behavior. Perhaps you have sinned, committed an offense, or violated a relationship, and you deeply regret your action. These situations usually generate guilt which leads to one of two responses—condemnation or conviction. If guilt becomes unhealthy, it develops into feelings of condemnation"

"What negative thoughts are you allowing to shape who you are and what you believe?"

Shame, though frequently confused with guilt, condemnation, and conviction, is different. Unlike guilt, shame is not a response to something you have done, but a response to who and what you perceive yourself to be. Shame is the energy behind feelings of inferiority, which entice us to compare ourselves with others. Shame is an inner sensing of defectiveness that colors our emotions and relationships and drives us toward self-depreciating behavior.

Take a quick survey of some of your lifestyle patterns that might indicate a stronghold of shame. Here are some examples:

Anger: frustrated with everything, blaming others, and not taking responsibility

† **Condemnation/ depression**: feeling condemned and guilty; in despair

† **Apologetic**: always apologizing, taking blame, or belittling yourself

† **Perfectionism**: always needing to have things right, perfect; very controlling

† **Passivity**: incapable of functioning in life or taking responsibility; not caring

† **Driving & Striving**: trying to prove your worth; overachieving, but also failing

† **Religious**: acting religious, presenting yourself as righteous, holy

The effects of shame are innumerable and can lead to crippling and destructive behaviors. Breaking free from shame is almost always a process, but it begins with a breakthrough and often recognizing the root causes. Consider some of these root causes for shame and the grip this stronghold may have had upon your life:

† Rejection

† Absence of real meaningful love

† Abandonment, neglect

† Any form of abuse—physical, verbal, sexual, religious

† Birth deformity, physical disability, speech, or learning problems

† Constant criticism or threats to perform well

† Unjust discipline, favoritism

† Embarrassment over physical appearance, parents, finances, living conditions, intelligence

† Being born a girl when parents wanted a boy or vice versa

† Shame by association—family lifestyle patterns of alcoholism, drugs, crime

One can be enabled by the Spirit to see the lie of shame and the truth of forgiveness, but there is often a lifetime of behavior and attitudes that must progressively be brought into alignment with the truth of who we are in Christ. Even if our actions have hurt others and ourselves, Jesus has completely forgiven us, if we will receive His forgiveness. His forgiveness is not just a covering of the sin, but a complete removal and cleansing. Give Him all of your shame and guilt and receive the absolute, complete forgiveness and cleansing that He paid for at Calvary.

IN SUMMARY

2 Corinthians 10:3-5 makes it clear that we are in a very real war. And the weapons given to us are mighty in God to pull down EVERY stronghold, EVERY mindset, EVERY belief, and EVERY wrong imagination. EVERY thing that lifts itself up against and in opposition to the Truth, bringing EVERY thing into captivity in obedience to Christ!

Setting our minds on things above, having a right perspective, being free from shame and guilt, and knowing our true identity in Christ is His utmost desire for us, His children. He has made it ALL possible because of His love for you and me.

♥ TAKE IT TO HEART

Here are five *"Steps"* to pulling down strongholds and ungodly beliefs. Take time to move through each one and follow through in prayer (below), thanking God for your healing and the new freedom that is yours.

1. Identify the stronghold or ungodly belief. Ask the Holy Spirit to reveal any patterns, strongholds, or ungodly beliefs.

2. Write down all the negative self-talk and evidence that the devil uses against you.

3. Repent of believing those lies, ungodly beliefs, and ask God to forgive you.

4. Receive His forgiveness. Then write down the truth and what the Word/ God says.

5. Start meditating on the truth, replacing the strongholds and lies with the truth.

⚛ TAKE IT TO GOD

Dear God, please reveal to me any and all strongholds, thoughts, and ungodly beliefs that have taken hold and are affecting my life in a negative way. Forgive me for agreeing with these lies and allowing them to direct my life. I choose this day to break all agreements with these strongholds, negative thoughts, and ungodly beliefs. I release these to You and ask that You bring Your beliefs and actions within my heart, mind and soul into alignment with Your Word. This day, I start believing the truth so I can be totally free, as You have promised! In Jesus's name, Amen.

Setting Our Minds on the Right Things

In the following passage, the Apostle Paul paints a picture of two distinct groups—those who live according to the flesh and those who live according to the Spirit.

> "For those who live according to the flesh set their minds on the things of the flesh, but those who live according to the Spirit, the things of the Spirit. For to be carnally minded is death, but to be spiritually minded is life and peace. Because the carnal mind is enmity against God; for it is not subject to the law of God, nor indeed can be. So then, those who are in the flesh cannot please God." Romans 8:5-8

It's important to understand that Paul is not writing about two types of Christians, but rather about how non-Christians differ from true Christians. While it's true that immature believers may yet live according to the flesh (Romans 7:14-25), and even mature believers at times yield to the flesh (Romans 8:12; Gal. 5:17), that is not what Paul is describing here. Paul is describing in these passages the spiritual condition of unbelievers when he refers to those living "according to the flesh," and which are characterized by death. Those who are living "according to the Spirit," however, are believers characterized by life and peace (Romans 8:6). The *nature* of each group determines their present behavior and their final destiny. Jesus made it very clear that there is only one track for the Christian life (Mark 3:34-38)!

> *"To live according to the Spirit means to be...determined by God's awakening."*

To be *according to* the flesh means to live under the flesh, to make it your rule, or to obey it. To live *according to* the Spirit means to be, "ruled and determined by God's awakening, regenerating, illuminating presence; characterized by the fact that He dwells in [us]" (H.C.G. Moule, 1903). Paul makes it clear that the phrase, "according to the flesh," not only means thought and understanding, but it includes the affections, the emotions, the desires, and the objects of pursuit. It's our mindset.

As true believers, the great challenge alongside the weight of being conformed to His image is the responsibility of setting our minds on the things of the Spirit. That means that we have to wage a battle in our thought life. We engage in an unseen war to set our mind on the *right things*--the things of the Spirit.

Unfortunately, the devil knows we are called to wage war against the flesh, and he will do everything possible to get our minds set on the flesh. The passage in Romans makes it abundantly clear that the way a person thinks is intimately related to the way that person lives, whether in Christ, in the Spirit and by faith, or in the flesh, in sin, and in spiritual death. A man's thinking and striving cannot be seen in isolation from the overall direction of his life; the latter will be reflected in the aims which he sets himself. The mind focused on the flesh leads to death. This happens when we put our focus on circumstances and problems surrounding us instead of on God and the truth of His Word.

We must pull down the strongholds in our mind, or we will never experience the freedom and victory that Jesus paid for us to have. Our thinking must be transformed and literally re-programmed by and through the Word of God. We must intentionally and actively set our minds on the Spirit and on the things above (Colossians 3:2). As we confess the Word, pray, praise, worship, give thanks, bless, and honor the Lord in other ways, we find the freedom that is in Christ.

"If then you were raised with Christ, seek those things which are above, where Christ is, sitting at the right hand of God. Set your mind on things above, not on things on the earth. For you died, and your life is hidden with Christ in God. When Christ who is our life appears, then you also will appear with Him in glory." Colossians 3:1-4

"Finally, brethren, whatever things are true, whatever things are noble, whatever things are just, whatever things are pure, whatever things are lovely, whatever things are of good report, if there is any virtue and if there is anything praiseworthy— meditate on these things." Philippians 4:8

"You will keep him in perfect peace, whose mind is stayed on You, because he trusts in You." Isaiah 26:3

"And do not be conformed to this world, but be transformed by the renewing of your mind, that you may prove what is that good and acceptable and perfect will of God." Romans 12:2

Have you taken a serious look at how you spend your spare time? Do you spend it watching television or playing video games, texting, shopping, at the gym, or eating out? How would you compare that to time in the Word, serving the Body, praying, or fellowshipping with believers? Of course, we are not saying that every spare minute should be focused on

"Finally, brethren, whatever things are true ... noble ... just ... pure ... lovely ... whatever things are of good report, if there is anything praiseworthy— meditate on these things." Philippians 4:8

spiritual activities. We all need down time and have life responsibilities. But are you making a serious effort toward a biblical lifestyle and mindset?

Consider, as well, what was shared in the Chapter on *Love, Identity, and Purpose.* Are there some core battles in these areas that need to be addressed? Our primary warfare and hindrance to intimacy and a deeper walk with God is usually within the following categories:

† The love and acceptance of the Father.

† Our identity as a beloved child of God.

† Our purpose and destiny in Christ.

Christ came to set you free from the law of sin and death, so that you could walk *according to the Spirit* and not be conformed to the world but transformed! And those who practice right-thinking will receive tremendous blessings. Isaiah 26:3 again says, "You will keep him in perfect peace, whose mind is stayed on You."

Embracing Disciplines

The word *set* is an active word. It can also be translated as *seek* or *focus.* The KJV says, "Seek those things which are above" (Colossians 3:1). This does not happen by accident; it only happens through rigorous discipline. The most difficult problem we face is not *finding time* but convincing ourselves that (fill in the blank) is important enough to set aside the time. If you are not actively seeking things above, purposefully setting aside time to seek, then you won't be thinking in a heavenly manner. In Romans 12:2, Paul says, "Do not conform to the pattern of this world but be transformed by the renewing of your mind."(NIV) The sense is to stop conforming, or stop being pressed and molded into the pattern of this world.

If you are not seeking things above, you are already being pressed and molded to look and think like the rest of the world.

In his book, *Celebration of Discipline*, Pastor Richard J. Foster examines the inward disciplines of prayer, fasting, meditation, and study in the Christian life; the outward disciplines of simplicity, solitude, submission, and service; the corporate disciplines of confession, worship, guidance, and celebration.

Regarding the disciplines of the spiritual life, Foster notes that they are not hard, yet in another sense, they are. The primary requirement is a longing after God, "As the deer pants [longingly] for the water brooks, so my soul pants [longingly] for You, O God" (Psalm 42:1-2-AMP). Perhaps somewhere in the hidden chambers of your life you have heard the call to a deeper, fuller life?

> *"The Lord leans in to hear your earnest cries for change and transformation."*

Be assured and encouraged to embrace the disciplines of this God-centered life, and He will be there for you every step of the way in your path to spiritual growth. His "yoke" is easy, and His burden is light. Come seeking and He will be found by you; He will answer. He leans in to hear your earnest cries for change and transformation. The promise is that the Holy Spirit will empower you to succeed in these endeavors, building into your life the practices of a deeper inward walk in the midst of normal everyday activities.

IN SUMMARY

The admonition found in Romans 8:5-8 would seem to be a very challenging one. Not only does it mean thoughts and understanding, but it includes the affections, the emotions, the desires, and the objects of pursuit and attention. Of course, most of us would agree that the world is insane in its fleshly offerings, daily calling out to us to satisfy some desire or lust. But do those *things* really provide lasting results, pleasure, and happiness?

God has given us the remedy for joylessness, lack, poverty, brokenness, and the void within the human heart. He says to set our minds on things above, in order to be renewed in our thinking, enabling us to focus on that which is good, right, and pure, while keeping our minds and hearts stayed on Him. In this, we will find lasting peace and joy.

It's critical that we embrace the disciplines of our inner spiritual life. They will bring us into harmony (peace) with the Spirit of God, others, and ourselves. It's a place of wholeness and well worth the journey.

♥ TAKE IT TO HEART

This exhortation and work of *setting your mind on things above* is a lifelong process that involves deep growth and has great rewards. To be sure, it's a journey that you'll want to take. Begin by honestly asking yourself these questions: *Do I set my mind on the things of the Spirit or on the things of the flesh? What is my daily focus? What are the areas over which I worry and stress the most? What direction am I heading?* Then, prayerfully take time to invite the Holy Spirit to speak to you about those things. Ask Him about the disciplines He wants to bring into your world.

⟨⟩ TAKE IT TO GOD

Dear God, I realize that, in some areas, my heart has been focused on things of this world and the flesh—not on those things that bring true significance, joy, or what You desire. My reality has been tainted by the culture and society in which I live and, in many ways, does not reflect Your Kingdom. I ask You to forgive me for putting other things first and over You and not setting my mind on things above. I ask that You would reveal those areas where I need to change. Search my heart and lead me in Your Truth. In Jesus's name, Amen.

Trauma and Inner Healing

*T*rauma is a wound inflicted by sudden, physical injury or emotional shock that causes long-term damage to our spirit, soul, and/or body. The enemy is always trying to invade, ambush, and take advantage of us, and trauma is an open door through which he gains access to us.

Although everyone experiences fear at times, it is one of the enemy's main tactics and is almost always associated with trauma. He uses traumatic events in our lives to open doors to the spirit of fear and anxiety. The enemy tries to make us afraid not only of him, but the spirit of fear brings all sorts of other spirits with it to afflict us.

In His Word, God has told us over one-hundred times not to be afraid. He tells us not to fear because He is in control. He is our refuge and strength. Fear is the opposite of faith, which is what connects us to God and His promises. Faith is the *currency* of the Kingdom of

"God has told us in His Word over 100 times to not be afraid!"

God. Likewise, the enemy uses fear, which motivates and stimulates the kingdom of darkness. Therefore, the enemy tries to get us to be afraid and frightened, which opens the door for him to attack us.

Are you experiencing excessive fear, anxiety, worry, stress, etc.? Are you a controlling person? Do you fear man or poverty? Are you extremely driven or stubborn? In 2 Timothy 1:7, God's word reminds us clearly that, "For God has not given us a spirit of fear, but of power and of love and of a sound mind." 1 John 4:18 tells us that, "There is no fear in love; but perfect love casts out fear, because fear involves torment. But he who fears has not been made perfect in love." Jesus is perfect love.

Conditions that can Cause Trauma

- † Abuse (physical, mental, or verbal)
- † Accidents
- † Violence
- † Physical attack
- † Rape
- † Being dominated through control
- † Excessive fear
- † Divorce
- † Loss of a loved one
- † Near death experience
- † Problems with your birth
- † Trauma to your mother while you were in the womb
- † Surgery or medical procedures of any kind

Rejection is another tactic of the enemy and the very genuine pain of it can cause trauma. Rejection is the absence of real, meaningful love. There may have been (or continues to be) very real circumstances in your life that caused rejection. These may have occurred during conception, development, or birth. Hurtful situations may have happened throughout childhood; there may have been experiences in school or college that caused great pain. The possibility of generational issues is something we have addressed, and are a legitimate source of trauma: death, disability, divorce, accidents, and loss. There is no limit to the potential for trauma from rejection and the strongholds created by it. *Healing the Brokenhearted* is a resource that has been provided for you in **Appendix C**, which will give more insight into these areas. Please read through it.

When a message of rejection is driven into the heart and allowed to infect the core beliefs, a person can suffer for many years with inner torment. Healing the wounds of rejection can seem far away or impossible, as the lies are driven deeper. Even Jesus lamented the loss of relationship and rejection with the people of Israel (Luke 13:34), expressing how He yearned to gather their children together. But there is HOPE. God has made a way for those wounds of rejection to be healed.

Inner Healing

Even though the enemy deals many blows to God's people, Jesus has made provision for our healing by taking our pain and hurt upon Himself at the Cross. The enemy causes us great emotional and mental pain and then wants us to blame God. Many of these attacks come through people who are, or should be, very close to us. God has provided physical, emotional, and spiritual healing for us through Jesus and His ministry, by the power of the Holy Spirit and the work of the Cross.

"He is despised and rejected by men, a Man of sorrows and acquainted with grief. And we hid, as it were, our faces from Him; He was despised, and we did not esteem Him. Surely He has borne our griefs and carried our sorrows; Yet we esteemed Him stricken, smitten by God, and afflicted. But He was wounded for our transgressions, He was bruised for our iniquities; the chastisement for our peace was upon Him, and by His stripes we are healed." Isaiah 53:3-5

What a wonderful passage! Jesus took our pain and suffered for us at the Cross. It was for us. He was despised and rejected so we could be "accepted in the Beloved" (Ephesians 1:6). Isaiah 53:4 says, He has "*borne* our griefs," which means, "to lift, to bear, to take our griefs." Isaiah says that He *carried*, which means, "to carry or to take up our sorrows." The word *sorrows* can be translated "pain." He was bruised for our iniquities and the punishment for our peace was upon Him. God provided complete healing for our hurts and pain through Jesus's sacrifice on the Cross. We, however, must make the exchange by giving Him our hurts and pain, then receive His healing.

The most remarkable promise is found in Luke 4:18-19: "The Spirit of the Lord is upon Me, because He has anointed Me to preach the gospel to the poor; He has sent Me to heal the brokenhearted, to proclaim liberty to the captives and recovery of sight to the blind, to set at liberty those who are oppressed."

This promise is first recorded and declared in Isaiah 61:2-3: "To proclaim the acceptable year of the Lord, and the day of vengeance of our God; to comfort all who mourn, to console those who mourn in Zion, to give them beauty for ashes, the oil of joy for mourning, the garment of praise for the spirit of heaviness; that they may be called trees of righteousness, the planting of the Lord, that He may be glorified."

Disappointment with God

"And when John had heard in prison about the works of Christ, he sent two of his disciples and said to Him, 'Are you the coming One, or do we look for another?' Jesus answered and said to them, 'Go and tell John the things which you hear and see: The blind see and the lame walk; the lepers are cleansed and the deaf hear; the dead are raised up and the poor have the gospel preached to them. And blessed is he who is not offended because of Me.'" Matthew 11:2-6

Have you ever been disappointed with God? Would you call this being "offended"? Most of us would never say we were *angry*. But, if we were honest, we would have to say that we have been upset because God did not heal us or one of our loved ones. Maybe a lot of prayer and conversation went into a dire situation, and it seemed that He did not help us in that time of need.

Make no mistake about it—the devil is always trying to get us to be angry and disappointed with God! In the garden, Adam blamed God for the woman that He had given him, who *caused* him to sin. The issue is that when we blame God for our problems, where do we go to receive help? In truth, God is not causing our problems. It is sin in us and in other people that cause us problems. If you have blamed God or believe that God has let you down, then please take some time to process through this, and ask God to reveal the root of the disappointment.

Only the Holy Spirit can heal the wounds of the past. We need to ask the Holy Spirit to remove the pain and trauma of past memories as we repent of all judgment and all unforgiveness. Pain in the soul can help us to identify areas that need healing, just as natural pain can reveal a physical issue. Ask the Holy Spirit to heal the memories of what happened by taking away the hurt and pain associated with those memories. Don't waste your pain or your sorrows even one more day by holding on to it. Release it and step into the healing God has promised you.

Many times, the Holy Spirit, by the gifts of the Spirit, will give you assurance that He knows your specific situation(s) and is able to address and remove your hurt. He is not restrained by time and space because He is Spirit; by His power He can truly heal the wounds. Trust in His power to bring healing to the past and let Him remove all your hurts and pain. God can and does heal and redeem our past hurts and trauma, turning them into weapons for us to use against the enemy.

IN SUMMARY

Trauma is a marked kind of suffering—the kind that overwhelms one's ability to cope. It's a whole category of wounds that cripple precious people. It's a wound that buries itself deep in our consciousness and subconsciousness. It can be a tragedy, at times, too heavy for us. It happens in the past but asserts itself over and over in the present.

The Good News is that we have a loving Father and a Savior who came to heal the broken, the wounded, the prisoner, the sorrowful, the downcast, and the poor, offering complete freedom and forgiveness from every place of pain. No trauma is bigger than God—not one!

♥ TAKE IT TO HEART

You may want to review Chapter 1: *Love, Identity, and Purpose* for more understanding of the places of hurt, wounding, or disappointment. The process of walking through inner healing* begins with acknowledging the events and areas of pain. Write them down. Then ask the Holy Spirit to bring anything out of the darkness and into His light. Just know that He is here with you and will lovingly, compassionately, and tenderly guide you through prayer, through repentance and forgiveness, and into His presence for your ultimate healing and freedom.

† Ask God to reveal the memory or hurt that contains the starting point of your pain.

† Listen and watch for the Lord to show you that event.

† Dialogue with the Lord and share with Him about your pain and your feelings.

† Invite Jesus into that memory. Watch for His presence and what He says or does.

† Release and give Him your pain and hurt.

† Make the exchange; receive His healing and breathe in new freedom.

TAKE IT TO GOD

Dear God, I ask You to reveal all trauma in my life that has opened a door for the enemy. By the power of the Holy Spirit, please heal the hurt and pain inflicted upon me through (list every occurrence of trauma). Lord, I ask You to bind up my broken heart and bring true healing to my soul. Set me free from the hurt and pain of past disappointments and redeem it for good. Bring beauty from the ashes, joy instead of mourning, praise in exchange for heaviness.

Thank you for Your forgiveness. May I now experience and live a grace-filled and fruitful life, to Your glory and the delight of my soul, as a beloved child of God. In Jesus's name, Amen.

---

*If you have been a victim of abuse and would like to receive more extensive ministry for trauma or inner healing, we recommend *Restoring the Foundations Ministry*. Information and locations can be found at www.rtfi.org

Realm of Darkness

You may be familiar with the term *occult* or the phrase *realm of the occult* that describes the supernatural, hidden, and mysterious realm of information, activity, and power that operates outside of God and the Trinity. Occultism is strictly forbidden in Scripture and condemned by God. Any time a person tries to gain entrance into the supernatural, spiritual realm through illegitimate means, he or she is practicing occult activity. People involved in occultism attempt to access the spirit realm through the devil and his counterfeit means, instead of going to God and seeking knowledge, truth, and the supernatural through His Holy Spirit. A very clear explanation of the seriousness of occult activity can be found in Deuteronomy 18:9-14 and Revelation 21:8; 22:15.

If you have been involved in any form of fortune telling, tarot cards, palm reading, Ouija boards, astrology, séances, or anything that involves seeking to know the future from any source other than God, then you have been, or are currently, involved in the occult. If you have participated in any form of witchcraft (casting spells, blood pacts, black or white magic, mind games, etc.), you have been involved in the occult and have given the enemy legal access to you. This can have damaging influences on your life and the lives of your descendants. You may have never been directly involved in the occult, but because of the sins of your ancestors, you could have inherited psychic abilities or familiar spirits.

It's very important to be on the alert concerning our children. The devil is subtly indoctrinating them to feel comfortable with witchcraft and sorcery. Many children's video games, movies, television shows, and books romanticize occult activity, by either making it seem powerful or by intriguing their curiosity. They become desensitized to the demonic realm and are thereby lulled into opening the door to the enemy's activity.

Any level of involvement in cults or false religions opens the door for the enemy to attack you and bring a curse into your life. All activity or participation in occultism needs to be renounced, and repentance needs to take place, even for groups such as these: Christian Science, Unitarianism, Buddhism, Islam, Hare Krishna, Mormonism, Jehovah's Witnesses, New Age, Hinduism, Freemasonry, fraternal organizations, and other false religions. In addition, if you have been active, or are active, in any of the following areas, you need to realize that the enemy is trying to draw you deeper into the occult:

† participating in any counterfeit religion

† allowing yourself to be hypnotized

† consulting mediums, spiritual guides, or channelers

† using mind-altering drugs

† being drawn to any occult phenomena

† obsessively wearing black or gothic attire

† being overly intrigued by death

† thinking about suicide

† religiously listening to heavy metal rock music

In the Old Testament, we are told about when Lucifer fell (Ezekiel 28; Isaiah 14), and that he took one-third of all of the angels with him. Although we believe these are the demons Jesus addresses, he never really discussed their origin. Even so, we do know that they are part of the kingdom of darkness. Part of Jesus's ministry was casting out demons and then He gave His disciples authority to cast out demons, too. We have already looked at spiritual warfare and the total victory of Christ for us. This is where we are rightly positioned— Jesus has all authority and has commissioned us to represent Him on earth to do the same things He did.

"Jesus went about all Galilee, teaching in their synagogues, preaching the gospel of the kingdom, and healing all kinds of sickness and all kinds of disease among the people. Then His fame went throughout all of Syria; and they brought to Him all sick people who were afflicted with various diseases and torments, and those who were demon-possessed, epileptics, and paralytics; and He healed them..."

Matthew 4:23-34

"And when He had called His twelve disciples to Him, He gave them power over unclean spirits, to cast them out, and to heal all kinds of sickness and all kinds of disease. And as you go, preach, saying, 'The kingdom of heaven is at hand.' Heal the sick, cleanse the lepers, raise the dead, cast-out demons. Freely you have received, freely give."

Matthew 10:1, 7-8

"Then one was brought to Him who was demon-possessed, blind and mute; and He healed him, so that the blind and mute man both spoke and saw. And all the multitudes were amazed and said, 'Could this be the Son of David?' Now when the Pharisees heard it, they said, 'This fellow does not cast out demons except by Beelzebub, the ruler of the demons.' But

Jesus knew their thoughts and said to them: 'Every kingdom divided against itself is brought to desolation, and every city or house divided against itself will not stand. If Satan casts out Satan, he is divided against himself. How then will his kingdom stand? And if I cast out demons by Beelzebub, by whom do your sons cast them out? Therefore, they shall be your judges. But if I cast out demons by the Spirit of God, surely the kingdom of God has come upon you. Or how can one enter a strong man's house and plunder his goods, unless he first binds the strong man? And then he will plunder his house. He who is not with Me is against Me, and he who does not gather with Me scatters abroad.'" Matthew 12:22-30

"And He said to them, 'Go into all the world and preach the gospel to every creature. He who believes and is baptized will be saved; but he who does not believe will be condemned. And these signs will follow those who believe: In My name they will cast out demons; they will speak with new tongues; they will take up serpents; and if they drink anything deadly, it will by no means hurt them; they will lay hands on the sick, and they will recover.'" Mark 16:15-18

"Now it happened, as we went to prayer, that a certain slave girl possessed with a spirit of divination met us, who brought her masters much profit by fortune-telling. This girl followed Paul and us, and cried out, saying, 'These men are the servants of the Most High God, who proclaim to us the way of salvation.' And this she did for many days. But Paul, greatly annoyed, turned and said to the spirit, 'I command you in the name of Jesus Christ to come out of her.' And he came out that very hour." Acts 16:16-18

We don't believe a Christian can be demon possessed. The correct Greek translation for possessed actually means to be harassed, afflicted, or tormented. So, while the devil cannot possess a Christian, demonic spirits do much to harass, torment, or afflict the believer.

Resisting the Devil

By this time, you should have most, if not all, the open doors (legal ground) closed to the enemy. Now it is time to resist the enemy and take authority over his evil ways. James 4:7 says, "Therefore, submit to God. Resist the devil and he will flee from you." Although the devil cannot snatch believers away from Christ (1 John 5:18), the enemy is still working to cause division among believers, rendering them ineffective in their testimony, and damaging their relationship with God. Because of this reality, we are called to "resist the devil." We are to stand firm and oppose the adversary of God's people.

"We are to stand firm and oppose the adversary of God's people."

Remember that Jesus came to set us free. He cast out demons and told his disciples to do the same. That's us—we are Christ's disciples and have all the authority, in Him, to stand against the kingdom of darkness.

> "He who sins is of the devil, for the devil has sinned from the beginning. For this purpose the Son of God was manifested, that He might destroy the works of the devil."
>
> 1 John 3:8

> "...God anointed Jesus of Nazareth with the Holy Spirit and with power, who went about doing good and healing all who were oppressed by the devil, for God was with Him."
>
> Acts 10:38

We have covered in Chapters 5 and 6, the open doors, behaviors, ungodly beliefs, generational patterns, and strongholds which could have brought demonic activity and oppression into your life. If you have not walked through those prayers and dealt with this realm of darkness, let me encourage you to go back through the information and do so now.

PRAYER

> *Dear God, please show me every open door in my life that has allowed the enemy to have access to me. Help me to turn to You in humility and repentance and close those doors so that I can be free. In Jesus's name, Amen."*

Below is a chart listing root spirits and associated effects of these spirits, either operating in your life or as something you've seen as a generational pattern. Take a moment to read through the list and highlight any of the areas that are patterns which you see in your generational line.

As you go through each section, repent for your participation, or your family's participation, in that behavior. In the name of Jesus, close the doors to the demonic spirit, commanding and declaring every demonic spirit assigned to carry out a generational pattern as powerless, rendering it to the power of Jesus Christ. After you close the door, pray the Godly replacement for that area using the verses identified. Luke 11:24-26 says, "When an unclean spirit goes out of a man, he goes through dry places, seeking rest; and finding none, he says, 'I will return to my house from which I came.' And when he comes, he finds it swept and put in order. Then he goes and takes with him seven other spirits more wicked than himself, and they enter and dwell there; and the last state of that man is worse than the first." In order to fill the area vacated by the demonic spirit, we declare the Godly replacement based on what God's word says.

Do this with each of the root spirits until you've renounced them all. Find someone with whom you can pray these prayers in agreement who has a heart to see you walk in freedom. It is scripturally based and very beneficial. Occasionally, some of the root spirits are not going to want to be evicted, so it may take some warfare. Don't grow weary, for in the end you will reap a reward. Freedom is worth every step you take.

Below is a sample for praying against the spirit of fear. Use this guide as you pray through all the sections on the chart.

> *In the name of Jesus, I rebuke the spirit of fear and every manifestation of fear including fear of abandonment, anxiety, worry, fright, fear of death, and fear of failure (name all the manifestations that apply to you). I command that every demonic spirit assigned to carry out a spirit of fear is now assigned to dry places. You have no place in me. I am covered with the blood of the lamb Jesus Christ, and every door opened to you is now closed in Jesus's name. In its place, I declare God's perfect love. "There is no fear in love; but perfect love casts out fear, because fear involves torment. But he who fears has not been made perfect in love" (1 John 4:18). "For God hasn't given me a spirit of fear, but of power and love and a sound mind." (2 Timothy 1:7). Amen.*

SPIRIT/BONDAGE CHART

INFIRMITY - LUKE 13:11		DIVINATION-ACTS 16:16-17	
__ allergies	__ high blood pressure	__ astrology	__ crystal balls/8 balls
__ arthritis	__ sinus trouble	__ seances	__ palm reading/
__ asthma	__ stroke	__ channeling	tarot cards
__ cancer	__ viruses	__ Satanism	__ hypnosis/TM
__ diabetes	__ weakness/feebleness	__ fortunetelling	__ Ouija boards
__ fungus	__ female problems	__ demonic games	__ Freemasonry
__ heart disease	__ male problems	__ horoscopes	__ rebellion
__ undiagnosed illness	__ lingering disorders	__ witchcraft	__ independence
		__ illegal drugs	__ manipulation
			__ abuse of legal drugs
REPLACE WITH: LIFE, PHYSICAL HEALING		**REPLACE WITH:** TONGUES, PROPHECY GIFTS OF THE HOLY SPIRIT, OBEDIENCE	

FEAR - 2 TIMOTHY 1:7		BONDAGE - ROMANS 8:15	
__ abandonment	__ performance	ADDICTION TO:	
__ anxiety	__ phobias	__ possessions	__ soul ties
__ worry	__ rejection	__ alcohol or drugs	__ co-dependency
__ faithlessness	__ viruses	__ cigarettes	__ anorexia
__ fright	__ idleness	__ work	__ bulimia
__ inferiority	__ shyness	__ computers	__ other addictions:
__ insanity	__ tension/stress	__ TV or video games	
__ nightmares	__ timidity	__ sex	
__ self-rejection	__ torment		
__ inadequacy			
(circle) fear of: Death, Failure, Poverty, Success, Authority, the Opposite			
REPLACE WITH: PERFECT LOVE 1 JOHN 1:4; 2 TIMOTHY 1:7; POWER LOVE & SOUND MIND		**REPLACE WITH:** SPIRIT OF ADOPTION, SONSHIP, LIBERTY	

WHOREDOM - HOSEA 4:2		HAUGHTINESS - PROVERBS 16:18-19	
__ adultery	__ child molestation	__ arrogant	__ prone to gossip
__ incest	__ masturbation	__ boastful	__ judgemental
__ exhibitionism	__ pornography	__ contentious	__ prejudiced
__ illegitimacy	__ voyeurism	__ controlling	__ mocking
__ molestation	__ molestation	__ critical	__ feelings of superiority:
__ seduction	__ multi-partner orgies	__ dictatorial	__ self-righteous
__ bestiality	__ rape	__ domineering	__ rude
	__ lust	__ proud/egotistical	__ given to vanity
	__ worshiping anything above God		
(CIRCLE) IDOLATRY OF: Money, Possessions, Position, Power			
REPLACE WITH: PURITY, HOLINESS		**REPLACE WITH:** HUMILITY	

PERVERSENESS - ISAIAH 19:14		ANTICHRIST	
__ homosexuality	__ lovers of self	__ opposes the Bible	__ suppresses ministries
__ multi-partner orgies	__ polygamy	__ martyrs the saints	__ causes church splits
__ sadomasochism	__ abnormal crankiness	__ gives up on	__ takes God's place
__ sexual deviation	__ stubbornness	Christianity	
__ error (esp. religious)	__ twisted thinking	__ blasphemes the	
__ teaching false	__ unreasonableness	Holy Spirit &	
doctrine		His gifts	
__ following false		__ harasses and	
teachers		persecutes the	
		believers	
		__ opposes Christ's	
		deity and humanity	
		__ rationalizes power	
		of God	
REPLACE WITH: HOLINESS		REPLACE WITH: ANOINTING OF THE HOLY SPIRIT	

DEAFNESS & DUMBNESS - MARK 9:25 - 27		HEAVINESS - ISAIAH 61:3	
__ convulsions	__ diseases of eyes/ears	__ abnormal grief or	__ loneliness
__ insanity	__ grinding of teeth	sorrow	__ defilement
__ epilepsy	__ schizophrenia	__ sadness	__ wounded spirit
__ seizures	__ accidents with water/	__ depression	__ self-pity
__ stupor	fire	__ discouragement/	__ unjustified guilt
	__ suicidal thoughts/	despair	__ rejection
	attempts	__ broken-heartedness	
		__ hopelessness	
REPLACE WITH: HEARING PEACE & RIGHT THINKING		REPLACE WITH: JOY, GARMENTS OF PRAISE	

LYING - 2 CHRONICLES 18:22		JEALOUSY - NUMBERS 5:14	
__ telling lies	__ feeling like hypocrite	__ anger or rage	__ unnatural competition
__ deception	__ poor self-image	__ hatred	__ self-centeredness
__ exaggeration	__ strong delusions	__ insecurity	__ covetousness
__ profanity	__ vain imaginations	__ cruelty	__ suspicion/distrust
__ emotionalism	__ condemnation	__ murder	__ wanting revenge
		__ divorce	__ jealousy
		__ hard-heartedness	__ divisive
		__ feeling of being	
(CIRCLE) THOUGHTS THAT YOU ARE: ugly, worthless,		less loved by God	
stupid, you will never get married; you will never change		than others	
REPLACE WITH: HONESTY		REPLACE WITH: LOVE OF GOD, BLESSING AND FORGIVING OTHERS	

ERROR - 1 JOHN 4:6		SLUMBER/STUPOR - ROMANS 11:8	
__ anorexia or bulimia	__ making wrong decisions	__ constant fatigue	__ passivity
__ intellectualism	__ confusion/deception	__ procrastination	__ withdrawing from life
__ immaturity	__ compromising	__ self-pity wishing you	__ blocked success
__ doubt/unbelief	__ irresponsibility	had never been born	
REPLACE WITH: TRUTH, RENEWED MIND		REPLACE WITH: LIFE, SOUL & SPIRIT AWAKEN TO LIFE	

Spiritual Housecleaning

It is critical for every believer to identify and free themselves and their family from things that defile the spiritual atmosphere of the home. Many families, even Christian families, suffer needlessly from unseen evil influences. This doesn't just happen. A demonically contaminated atmosphere is a result of *doors* that have been left open. As we have discussed, these are doors of sin—even the sins of previous residents and of past generations! And evil's grip is often maintained as a result of one's possessions.

Unfortunately, many things we have in our homes can have demonic origin: music, relics of false religions, books, magazines, videos, jewelry, seemingly innocent paintings, statues, sculptures, decorations or other works of art, objects of witchcraft (particularly from other countries), etc.

The following Scriptures give a biblical precedent for removing such objects from your possession or from your home:

> "And many who had believed came confessing and telling their deeds. Also, many of those who had practiced magic brought their books together and burned them in the sight of all. And they counted up the value of them, and it totaled fifty thousand pieces of silver. So, the Word of the Lord grew mightily and prevailed." Acts 19:18-20

> "You shall utterly destroy all the places where the nations which you shall dispossess served their gods, on the high mountains and on the hills and under every green tree. And you shall destroy their altars, break their sacred pillars, and burn their wooden images with fire; you shall cut down the carved images of their gods and destroy their names from that place. You shall not worship the Lord your God with such things." Deuteronomy 12:2-4

Ask the Holy Spirit to show you everything that is demonic in origin or that represents the demonic, the occult, or false religion. Then rid your home of those items. Give the Holy Spirit the liberty to reveal anything that may have ties to something harmful or evil. Your home should reflect the pure, peaceful presence of Christ. A defiled spiritual atmosphere will affect you, your relationships, your health, and even your success. But you can remove and eliminate the enemy's influence over your home, your life, and your family by this act of spiritual housecleaning. The result will be a sanctuary of peace and purity in which to dwell.

IN SUMMARY

We can be eternally grateful that the doors to our freedom are clearly marked and that we hold every *key* through the finished work of Christ on the Cross. Within this chapter, you have been given an understanding of the realm of darkness and what you need to do in order to break the power of the enemy and stand against his intrusion and tactics--lies, legal access, generational curses, sin, rebellion, the occult, and areas of demonic activity. By confessing and repenting, and then resisting and standing, we take personal responsibility for our walk and we find ourselves in the place of true freedom and empowerment—having all the keys we need to remain free.

♥ TAKE IT TO HEART

If you are feeling overwhelmed with the breadth of this subject or the content and information in this chapter, we understand. The works of the devil in our day and age are varied and complex. You may not have realized the presence or influence of demonic activity in your life or in the lives of those you love. Satan's reach has gained inroads into our minds, emotions, bodies, relationships, and culture. But just know that Jesus has already waged war against this kingdom of darkness and has won! Jesus has made a way for YOU to be victorious and walk out the freedom from all demonic activity or oppression. He came to undo the works of the devil (1 John 3:8). You have been given the opportunity to encounter our living and present God, who moves in power and authority to overcome the impact of living in a fallen world system.

⚡ TAKE IT TO GOD

Dear God, I turn from and renounce all false religion and all occult activity I have ever participated in, and I choose to turn to You. Please forgive me for all involvement, deliberate or innocent, in false religion, the occult, witchcraft, or any activity or belief that is contrary to You and Your Word. I ask You, Holy Spirit, to cut off all past illegal activity by the blood of Jesus and to cut off all callings, interferences, and harassment that have come from this involvement. I repent and ask Your forgiveness for being involved in these activities.

Lord, I want to know You, be conformed to Your image, and have my heart and life be a holy dwelling place for Your Spirit. I acknowledge that I need You and I humble myself before Your mighty hand. I ask You to release Your mercy and grace in my life. Thank you.

In Jesus's name, Amen.

Daily Walking it Out

SECURING YOUR FREEDOM

> Then you will know the truth, and the truth will set you free.
>
> John 8:32 NIV

What does it mean to be truly free? Throughout this book, you have been given the opportunity to repent, renounce, forgive, and receive forgiveness—all very important decisions and actions to secure your freedom in Christ. You have experienced some life-changing moments with God, and YOU know you will never be the same again!

Understanding what freedom means is important. You can add to this list, but here are a few significant exchanges that were made as you prayed and invited the Holy Spirit to transform your heart and life. You were and are delivered, rescued, set apart, released; no longer a slave, no longer a captive, free of guilt and condemnation; free from the lies of the enemy, you are free from the fear of evil or failure; you are free from judgments and inner vows; free from the debt of sin that was owed; free to love, free to live. You have had a renewal of your worth and value. You have a place in the family of God. You have a purpose, and an identity. You qualify for the inheritance that the Father has reserved for you. You are highly favored, and you are blessed to be a blessing to others! Totally free—INDEED!

Walking it Out is a choice that you will make daily, in order to maintain your freedom. The Lord is even more committed than you are to your success and blessing. The Holy Spirit will lead and guide you in these very practical and important steps:

1. Know God through His Word. Let His Word "become flesh," or become living and real in your heart (John 1:14). Discover the awesome love of the Father. Find out and believe who you are *in Christ*.

2. Set your mind on things above (Colossians 3:2). Your mindset will have to change and be renewed. Watch negative thoughts. Watch for condemnation and accusations toward yourself and toward God. These come from the enemy.

3. Embrace the Holy Spirit and trust Him to speak to you. He will never say anything contrary to God's Word. He does not condemn you. However, He will convict you of sin.

4. Remove anything that is part of the kingdom of darkness from your possession or from your home.

5. Treat all sin and disobedience as poison. Ask the Holy Spirit to reveal all areas of sin and become aware of things that would grieve Him.

6. Be quick to repent and receive forgiveness when you fail or sin. Confess your sin, receive forgiveness and be cleansed. 1 John 1:9 says, "If we confess our sins, He is faithful and just to forgive us our sins and to cleanse us from all unrighteousness."

7. Recognize the real enemy, which is not flesh and blood (people). We are in a war. It is not against people, but against the forces of the devil (Ephesians 6:12). Remember to:

† Submit to God (James 4:7).

† Resist the devil (1 Peter 5:8, 9). Take authority in Jesus's name.

† Put on the armor of God and enter into spiritual warfare (Ephesians 6:10-18).

† Take every thought captive to the obedience of Christ (2 Corinthians 10:3-6).

† Begin to walk in the Spirit, realizing that the flesh wars against the Spirit (Galatians 5:16, 17).

8. Become involved in a local church that understands and preaches the Word and the full counsel of God. Make it a priority to:

† **Submit** to the leadership, so that you can be under authority properly.

† **Attend** the local functions on a regular basis.

† **Read** and study the Bible.

† **Learn** to pray and grow in your prayer life.

† **Be accountable** to someone or a small group who can walk with you.

† **Develop friendships** and spend time together.

9. Express your thanksgiving to the Lord for your victory (2 Corinthians 2:14). Remember His benefits and healing, which has been granted to you.

10. Spend time in worship. Let your praise be the highway to joy and communion with the Lord (Rom.15:9-13).

"Rejoice always, pray without ceasing, in everything give thanks; for this is the will of God in Christ Jesus for you. Do not quench the Spirit. Do not despise prophecies. Test all things; hold fast what is good. Abstain from every form of evil." 1 Thessalonians 5:16-22

"Therefore by Him let us continually offer the sacrifice of praise to God, that is, the fruit of our lips, giving thanks to His name." Hebrews 13:15

"For with the heart one believes unto righteousness, and with the mouth confession is made unto salvation."

Romans 10:10

IN SUMMARY

Now that you've discovered what the Word of God says about who you are—believe it and repeat it! Make it your daily practice to confess the Word. Knowing, believing, and confessing the truth of God's Word will help you immensely. You have been given tools, steps, encouragement, and lots of Scriptures to guide you in this journey of faith and love. The most wonderful promise guaranteed in God's Word is that the Lord will never fail to walk with you every moment of every day.

♥ TAKE IT TO HEART

An extraordinary life has been offered to you. Jesus came that we might have life and that we might have it abundantly (John 10:10). But it's a choice. Throughout this book, you have chosen life and said, "Yes" to the One who came to set you free, bringing healing, and giving you a new perspective and outlook on life. The weight of this decision is found in these verses in the Bible—when we do not choose life, we are really choosing death.

"See, I have set before you today life and good, death and evil, in that I command you today to love the Lord your God, to walk in His ways, and to keep His commandments, His statutes, and His judgments, that you may live and multiply; and the Lord your God will bless you in the land which you go to possess... I have set before you life and death, blessing and cursing; therefore choose life, that both you and your descendants may live; that you may love the Lord your God, that you may obey His voice, and that you may cling to Him, for He is your life and the length of your days; and that you may dwell in the land which the Lord swore to your fathers, to Abraham, Isaac, and Jacob, to give them." Deuteronomy 30:15-20

He calls you to LIFE, to freedom, to hope, to purpose, to joy, and to love. You have heard His voice and received freedom. I know you'll daily continue to choose LIFE!

TAKE IT TO GOD

Dear God, in this solemn moment, I make the choice to follow You and to choose LIFE.

I thank You for the blessings and favor that are awaiting me, according to Your Word. May the reality and awareness of Your presence grow in my heart and in my soul as we journey together. I choose to fight the good fight, to finish the race, and keep the faith. I know that You'll see me through every storm and always bring me to a place of peace. I rest in the knowledge of Your never-failing love for me. With a grateful heart...I pray. In Jesus's name, Amen.

APPENDICES

YOUR TRUE IDENTITY AS A BELIEVER

The following statements summarize your Scriptural identity and position in Christ, forming the foundation for your freedom in Christ. The statements below are the TRUTH. What we have believed in the past are lies.

Read these statements* aloud often. If you are presently involved in a spiritual conflict, read these statements aloud at least once each day for thirty days. Let them get into your spirit. Meditate upon them until this is the *way you think*. Remember, the truth will set you free!

WHO AM I?

✝ I am what I am (1 Corinthians 15:10) . . . by the grace of God.

✝ I am the salt of the earth (Matthew 5:13).

✝ I am the light of the world (Matthew 5:14).

✝ I am a child of God (John 1:12).

✝ I am a branch of the true Vine (John 15:1-5).

✝ I am Jesus's friend (John 15:15).

✝ I am chosen and appointed by Christ to bear His fruit (John 15:16).

✝ I am a slave of righteousness (Romans 6:18).

† I am a slave of God (Romans 6:22).

† I am a child of God; He is my spiritual Father (Romans 8:14-15; Galatians 3:26; 4:6).

† I am a joint heir with Christ, sharing His inheritance with Him (Romans 8:17).

† I am a saint (1 Corinthians 1:2).

† I am a dwelling place of God. My body is the temple of the Holy Spirit (1 Corinthians 3:16; 6:19).

† I am a member of Christ's body (1 Corinthians 12:27, Ephesians 5:30).

† I am a new creation in Christ (2 Corinthians 5:17).

† I am reconciled to God and have been given the ministry of reconciliation (2 Corinthians 5:18).

† I am a child of God and one with others in Christ (Galatians 3:26, 28).

† I am an heir of God through Christ, because I am a child of God (Galatians 4:6, 7).

† I am God's workmanship, created in Christ for good works (Ephesians 2:10).

† I am a fellow citizen with the saints and members of God's family (Ephesians 2:19).

† I am a citizen of Heaven, seated in heavenly places in Christ Jesus (Philippians 3:20; Ephesians 2:6).

† I am hidden with Christ in God (Colossians 3:3).

† I am chosen of God, holy, and beloved (Colossians 3:12; 1 Thessalonians 1:4).

† I am a son or daughter of light and not of darkness (1 Thessalonians 5:5).

† I am a holy partaker of a heavenly calling (Hebrews 3:1).

† I am one of God's living stones, being built up in Christ as a spiritual house (1 Peter 2:5).

† I am a member of a chosen generation, a royal priesthood, a holy nation, and His own special people (1 Peter 2:9).

† I am a child of God, and I will be like Jesus when He is revealed (1 John 3:1, 2).

BECAUSE I AM IN CHRIST, BY THE GRACE OF GOD . . .

† I have been justified by faith and have peace with God (Romans 5:1).

† I am free from condemnation (Romans 8:1).

† I have received the Spirit of God, that I might know the things freely given to me by God (1 Corinthians 2:12).

† I have been bought with a price; I am not my own. I belong to God (1 Corinthians 6:19, 20).

† I have been established, anointed, and sealed by God in Christ; and I have been given the Holy Spirit as a guarantee of God's promises (2 Corinthians 1:20, 21).

† Since I have died, I no longer live for myself, but for Christ (2 Corinthians 5:14, 15).

† I have been made the righteousness of God in Christ (2 Corinthians 5:21).

† I have been crucified with Christ, and it is no longer I who live, but Christ lives in me; and the life I now live is in Christ (Galatians 2:20).

† I have been blessed with every spiritual blessing (Ephesians 1:3).

† I was predestined, determined by God, to be adopted as God's child (Ephesians 1:5).

† I am accepted in the Beloved (Ephesians 1:6).

† I have been redeemed and forgiven, according to the riches of His grace (Eph. 1:7, 8).

† I have been made alive together with Christ (Ephesians 2:4, 5).

† I have been raised up and seated in heavenly places in Christ (Ephesians 2:6).

† I have direct access to God by the Spirit (Ephesians 2:18).

† I may approach God with boldness and confidence through faith (Ephesians 3:12).

† I have been delivered from the power of darkness and transferred to the kingdom of Christ (Colossians 1:13).

† I have redemption and forgiveness through the blood of Jesus (Colossians 1:14).

† I am made complete in Christ (Colossians 2:10).

† I have been buried, raised, and made alive with Christ (Colossians 2:12, 13).

† I died with Christ and I have been raised up with Christ. My life is now hidden with Christ in God. Christ is now my life (Colossians 3:1-4).

† I have been given a spirit of power, love, and of a sound mind (2 Timothy 1:7).

† I have been saved and called with a holy calling, according to God's purpose and grace

† (2 Timothy 1:9, Titus 3:4-7).

† I can come boldly before the throne of grace to receive mercy and find grace to help in time of need (Hebrews 4:16).

† I have been given exceedingly great and precious promises by God, by which I am a partaker of God's divine nature (2 Peter 1:4).

*Adapted from Neil Anderson's **Victory Over the Darkness** © 2000 by Neil T. Anderson, published by Regal Books, Ventura, CA.*

FREEDOM FROM THE FLESH

"Therefore, if anyone is in Christ, he is a new creation; old things have passed away; behold, all things have become new."

2 Corinthians 5:17

At the Cross, the power of sin to operate in our lives was canceled once and for all. Because of that divine moment in time, now God enables us to live and reign in Him as we appropriate the truth of the Cross and the resurrection in our lives (Romans 5:17, 21). Our body of sin (the old man, our carnal nature, the flesh) has literally been rendered inoperative. Anyone who is in Christ is a brand-new creation. The words used here refer to something unprecedented and unimaginable. We become something that this world has never known.

But how do we walk this out? How do we kill the flesh and put to death the deeds of the flesh?

If we allow the deeds of the flesh to work in our lives, we will continue to open the door to the enemy. Therefore, we must put to death the deeds of the flesh and choose to put on the new—the image of Jesus. Romans 6:1-10 helps us understand that we were baptized into Christ's death. Since Jesus is no longer dead but risen in victory, we are also risen from death into life with Him, united (joined together) with Him in His death, and united with Him in His life. Therefore, we should live like we are joined to Him and walking in victory with Him.

> "What shall we say then? Shall we continue in sin that grace may abound? Certainly not! How shall we who died to sin live any longer in it? Or do you not know that as many of us as were baptized into Christ Jesus were baptized into His death? Therefore, we were buried with Him through baptism into death, that just as Christ was raised from the dead by the glory of the Father, even so we also should walk in newness of life. For if we have been united together in the likeness of His death, certainly we also shall be in the likeness of His resurrection, knowing this, that our old man was crucified with Him, that the body of sin might be done away with, that we should no longer be slaves of sin. For he who has died has been freed from sin. Now if we died with Christ, we believe that we shall also live with Him, knowing that Christ, having been raised from the dead, dies no more. Death no longer has dominion over Him. For the death that He died, He died to sin once for all; but the life that He lives, He lives to God." Romans 6:1-10

Paul answers his own question in Romans 6:2: "How can we who died to sin still live in it?" We can't. If we died to sin by being united with Jesus in his death, we can't stay married to sin. The faith that unites us to Christ disunites us from all competitors. The very faith that makes peace with God makes war on our sin. If you are not at odds with sin, you are not at home with Jesus, not because being at odds with sin makes you at home with Jesus, but because being at home with Jesus makes you at odds with sin. Selah. (Stop and think about that!)

> "Likewise you also, reckon yourselves to be dead indeed to sin, but alive to God in Christ Jesus our Lord. Therefore do not let sin reign in your mortal body, that you should obey it in its lusts. And do not present your members as instruments

of unrighteousness to sin, but present yourselves to God as being alive from the dead, and your members as instruments of righteousness to God."

Romans 6:11-13

"Knowing this, that our old man was crucified with Him, that the body of sin might be done away with, that we should no longer be slaves of sin." Romans 6:6

What are those things which are called sin? Colossians 3:5-10 lists a few: "Therefore, put to death your members which are on the earth: fornication, uncleanness, passion, evil desire, and covetousness, which is idolatry. Because of these things the wrath of God is coming upon the sons of disobedience, in which you yourselves once walked when you lived in them. But now you yourselves are to put off all these: anger, wrath, malice, blasphemy, filthy language out of your mouth. Do not lie to one another, since you have put off the old man with his deeds and have put on the new man who is renewed in knowledge according to the image of Him who created him."

You may be saying, "I don't know if I can really do this." SURE, YOU CAN! It has nothing to do with your power or ability. It has everything to do with His grace, His power, and His love. It is the understanding that the Holy Spirit raised Jesus from the dead and that the same Holy Spirit who raised Jesus from the dead lives in us. You may have failed in the past for a couple of reasons:1) You did not reckon yourself dead to sin or did not understand that you are no longer a slave to sin; 2) You tried in your own power to resist sin, but still found yourself consumed by it (Romans 7:14-24).

Other reasons? Probably.

"But if the Spirit of Him who raised Jesus from the dead dwells in you, He who raised Christ from the dead will also give life to your mortal bodies through His Spirit who dwells in you." Romans 8:11

"I have been crucified with Christ; it is no longer I who live, but Christ lives in me; and the life which I now live in the flesh I live by faith in the Son of God, who loved me and gave Himself for me." Galatians 2:20

"Now to Him who is able to do exceedingly abundantly above all that we ask or think, according to the power that works in us." Ephesians 3:20

"Do you not know that you are the temple of God and that the Spirit of God dwells in you?" 1 Corinthians 3:16

One final note. The daily practice of walking by the Spirit, waging war, and bringing death to sin in your life is the evidence and result of being justified by faith alone in Christ. And His blood and righteousness provide the unshakable ground of your sanctification and the VICTORY for your life.

YES! The exceeding greatness of His power toward us is in us— the Holy Spirit!

APPENDIX C

DECLARATION OF FAITH

This declaration of faith is effective when read out loud, declaring your faith in Jesus Christ, and appropriating all the victory in your life. It is not a one-time declaration, but it is particularly important as you are commanding demonic activity to cease in your life.

In the name of Jesus, this is my confession. I believe that:

† Jesus Christ is the virgin-born Son of God.

† He died on the Cross for my sins.

† He arose from death on the third day with victory over death, hell, and the grave.

† He ascended later into Heaven and is seated at the right hand of God, the Father.

† From His glorified position He sent His Holy Spirit to earth.

† At this moment He is interceding for me and for all the redeemed of the earth.

I now testify that:

† I have trusted Jesus Christ as my own personal Lord and Savior.

† He now resides in me by the Holy Spirit.

† He has fully forgiven me, completely justified me, and is continually sanctifying me daily.

† He has paid the penalty for all my sins: past, present, and future.

† He has won not only my forgiveness and justification through His death and resurrection, but my freedom as well.

† I am free in Him. I have a responsibility to be free and believe, think, pray, and act in freedom.

† I renounce the devil and all of his works in my life; I declare that I am now a slave of righteousness.

I now affirm that:

† My body is the Temple of the Holy Spirit and exists for His indwelling, control, and manifestations.

† I agree now to take back, in Jesus's name, all ground formerly given to satan and his evil spirits. I confess that they now have no legal place in me or power over me.

† He who is in me is greater than he who is in the world.

† Jesus was manifested to destroy the works of the evil one.

† Jesus spoiled principalities and powers and made an open spectacle of them on the Cross.

† I overcome by the blood of the Lamb, the word of my testimony, and I love not my life unto death.

† Father, I submit to Your Lordship over my life. I thank You for loving me, and I thank You for the victory of the Cross and the blood that was shed for me.

HEALING THE BROKENHEARTED

Healing the Brokenhearted

Causes	Produce	Wrong Responses & Open Doors	Results
• Lack of Love • Rejection • Abuse—Verbal, Physical • Neglect • Betrayal • Trauma • Original causes cannot be changed, but they can be healed.	• Longing to be loved • Hurt & Pain • Shame • Insecurity • Fear • Unhealed hurts & unmet needs fuel our pain. Pain is an indication that we have not fully forgiven from the heart, or haven't received healing from the Holy Spirit.	• Dishonoring parents • Anger / Unforgiveness • Judgments / Inner Vows • Curses • Occult / False Religion • Trauma • Soul Ties • Regardless of what was done to us, it is our wrong responses that open doors leading to bondage.	• Wrong Behaviors • Addictions • Controlling Fears • Critical and Angry • Unable to submit to authority • Sexual Sins • Legalism • These are all results of wrong responses. We must take personal responsibility for our actions. • Strongholds, faulty patterns of thinking • Victim Mentality • Defensiveness • Can't trust anyone • Hopelessness • Suicidal thoughts • We must pull down these negative patterns of thinking by God's Word.
• Broken heart	• Pain	• Sin	• Medicating the pain • Trying to find love **Wrong Thinking**

How To Receive Healing

Causes	Produce	Wrong Responses & Open Doors	Results
• Receive the love of the Father & His affirmation of our true identity as a son of God & join His purpose of advancing His Kingdom • Romans 8:15-17 • Romans 5:8	• Receive the healing ministry of the Holy Spirit • Luke 4:18 • Isaiah 53:3-5	• Take personal responsibility for wrong responses, call them sin and receive forgiveness • 1 John 1:9	• Reckon yourself dead to sin and alive to God • Present your members as slaves of righteousness • Romans 6:11-13 • Dismantle strongholds through the truth of God's Word • John 8:32 • 2 Corinthians 10:3-5

Focus on the Love of the Father

Let faith arise by abiding in His Word

RESOURCE LIST

The following resource materials are suggested to supplement your studies about freedom.

- † *The Cross is the Key* by Terry Moore
  JTerryMoore.org

- † *Battlefield of the Mind* by Joyce Meyer
  www.joycemeyer.org

- † *Blessings or Curses* by Derek Prince
  www.derekprince.com

- † *The Bruises of Satan* by Carroll Thompson
  www.carrollthompson.org

- † *Clearing the Land* by Geri McGhee
  www.abidinglifeministries.org

- † *Experiencing the Holy Spirit* by Robert Heidler
  www.gloryofzion.org

- † *Freedom From Your Past* by Jimmy Evans
  https://www.youtube.com/watch?v=-H97oaPb6uc

- † *Victory Over Darkness* (book) by Neil Anderson
  www.freedominchrist.com

- † *Victory Over Darkness* (study guide) by Neil Anderson
  www.freedominchrist.com

† *The Integrated Approach to Biblical Healing* by Chester and Betsy Kylstra

www.restoringthefoundations.org

† *Restoring the Foundations* by Chester and Betsy Kylstra

www.restoringthefoundations.org

† *Orphans No More* by Dudley Hall

www.kerygmaventures.com/

† *Celebration of Discipline* by Richard J. Foster

www.richardjfoster.com

ABOUT THE AUTHOR

 Terry Moore graduated from SMU with a degree in business administration. After graduating, Terry married his childhood sweetheart, Susan Stroube Moore, who also graduated from SMU's Class of 1973. Shortly thereafter, Terry began his career in commercial real estate and subsequently diversified into the oil & gas industry as an investor and an independent producer.

Terry and Susan became successful business owners, active in their church and community. In 1982, the couple attended a Christian Conference where they encountered the Lord in a life-changing way. The Moores then began a Bible Study in their home, which continued for four years and influenced many people who encouraged them to consider starting a church. In January 1987, Terry and Susan, along with several other couples from the Bible Study, founded Sojourn Church. This was a major shift for Terry who had never considered ministry as a career option. Under his leadership, the church continued to grow, resulting in the 1997 relocation to its current facility in Carrollton, Texas. As the membership increased with families from around the Metroplex, the Moores were instrumental in raising up leaders and planting new churches in the region.

For nearly three decades, Sojourn Church has been instrumental in coordinating and hosting conferences for thousands of participants locally and globally. Additionally, Terry and Susan partner with several local inner-city ministries, which feed the poor, offer recovery programs, provide after school programs and adult education for re-entry into mainstream society.

Terry spends much of his time preparing messages, meeting with leaders, and encouraging others. He has written a number of Bible studies designed to equip Christians to live victoriously. He serves on the board of several local ministries, as well as many international organizations.

Terry and Susan have traveled extensively around the world. They continue to be involved in a number of overseas missions where they equip pastors and church leaders with the life-changing power of Jesus Christ.

Terry is the Founding Pastor and an Elder of Sojourn Church. He and Susan have been married forty-seven years and have a son and daughter in-law who have two teenage children, and daughter and son-in-law who have three young daughters.

MORE TITLES AVAILABLE IN THE ADVANCED FOUNDATIONS SERIES

Basic Training—published in 2021

Cross is the Key—coming soon

Love, Identity & Purpose—coming soon

Hear and Obey—coming soon

Setting the Captives Free—coming soon

A video series for these titles is
available at jterrymoore.org

For more information on Free Indeed
or any title in the series, visit:
www.jterrymoore.org

Made in the USA
Coppell, TX
04 February 2023

12170914R00090